THE
SCIENCE OF WEALTH

By

J. A. HOBSON

First published in 1911

British Library Cataloguing-in-Publication Data
A catalogue record for this book is available
from the British Library

The tendency of all strong Governments has always been to suppress liberty, partly in order to ease the processes of rule, partly from sheer disbelief in innovation.

J. A. HOBSON

CONTENTS

PREFACE

THIS volume contains a study of the structure and working of the modern business world in which wealth is made and distributed as income to those who have made it or can lawfully get hold of it. It describes the ways in which the productive powers of Labour, Ability, Land, Capital, and Society are applied in the various trades, arts, and professions, for the production of material goods and services, and the ways in which the payment for this work is regulated and carried out. No knowledge of economic facts or principles is presumed, except such as every intelligent man or woman acquires in the ordinary experience of life.

So brief a presentation of so large a subject will suffer necessary defects. It will be apt to be too unqualified in statement and too dogmatic in mode of argument. It will shirk some important points of controversy.

Since the line of interpretation taken here has been more fully defended in a larger volume entitled *The Industrial System*, I may be permitted to refer to it those readers who may wish to follow out the argument in more detail.

J. A. HOBSON.

NOTE ON BOOKS

STUDENTS desiring to follow the growth of the Science of Wealth in this country will begin with Adam Smith's *Wealth of Nations*, following with Ricardo's *Principles*, and J. S. Mill's *Principles of Political Economy* for the "classical" theory. In Jevons' *Theory of Political Economy* they will find a challenge to the older theory, and a new interpretation of economic "value." The best authoritative statement of modern "orthodox" theory is in Marshall's *Principles of Economics* (Macmillan), while Philip H. Wicksteed's *Common Sense of Political Economy* (Macmillan) presents a valuable psychological interpretation.

A reliable brief account of the growth of the science may be found in L. L. Price's *Political Economy in England* (Methuen), whilst E. Cannan presents a very useful criticism of much of the earlier work in his *Theories of Production and Distribution* (P. S. King). In Foxwell's Introduction to Menger's *Right to the Whole Produce of Labour* is found an interesting account of the beginnings of socialistic theory in England, in connection with which Hyndman's *Economics of Socialism* and Bernstein's *Evolutionary Socialism* may be read.

For a fuller statement of the method of description and interpretation adopted in this volume I may refer to my *Evolution of Modern Capitalism* (Scott) and *The Industrial System* (Longmans). Among innumerable special studies of the facts and problems of modern industry, I would refer among the larger works to Booth's *Life and Labour in London* (Macmillan), and Rowntree's *Poverty* (Macmillan), Schloss's *Methods of Industrial Remuneration* (Williams and Norgate), Dr. Shadwell's *Industrial Efficiency* (Longmans), and Brassey and Chapman's *Work and Wages* (Longmans). But the largest ordered mass of information upon present-day industrial conditions lies in the Reports of the Poor Law Commission.

On Finance two excellent elementary textbooks may be found in Withers' *The Meaning of Money* (Methuen), and Armitage Smith's *Principles and Methods of Taxation* (Murray).

THE SCIENCE OF WEALTH

CHAPTER I

THE MEANING OF WEALTH

COMMON usage in the present day confines the term " Wealth " to things capable of being bought and sold, measuring the amount of wealth they represent by the quantity of money they would fetch in the market. When we think and speak of " a wealthy man," we reduce to terms of money all his saleable possessions, including not only the lands, buildings, machinery, materials, cash, he owns and employs for business purposes, together with the share certificates and other paper documents which give him claims upon the produce of the future, but also his house, furniture, pictures, books and other private possessions which he has no intention of selling. All have their market value and his " wealth " is the sum of these values.

The " wealth " of a nation may be estimated in a similar manner. Taken at any given time, it will consist of the total sum of marketable goods owned by the State and by the citizens who are the units of the nation. It will, of course, include some goods which lie abroad in foreign countries, and will exclude some goods which, though lying inside the country, belong to foreigners.

The wealth of Great Britain, thus conceived, will not include any money estimate of her geographical position or climate, or any other natural advantages which are of use for individual and commercial purposes. The Thames, as a business asset for the nation, will only rank as national wealth indirectly, in so far as it affords facilities to businesses engaged in the carrying trade. There are two good reasons for excluding these natural advantages from a business estimate of national wealth. In the first place, they are not for sale and no market valuation can be set on them. Secondly, if such a valuation of climate, position, harbourage, etc., were attempted, it would cause overlapping and duplication in the " national accounts," for all these natural advantages, utilized as they are for countless purposes in private businesses, would then be reckoned twice over.

Thus, whether we regard individuals or nations, it will be convenient for business purposes to confine " wealth " to marketable

articles taken at their market value. This
rule has its difficulties and its defects. Things
which are " wealth " in one place or at one
time are not wealth in another place or at
another time. When the population of a
country grows, much land which was not
wealth becomes wealth : water, air and
sunshine pass from " free " into marketable
goods in the rise of city rents. Though slave
labour is far less productive than free labour,
the emancipation of slaves in the United
States cancelled a vast amount of private
wealth.

Again, reckoning wealth by market prices
not merely implies a constant change in
the amount of wealth any particular goods
represent, but changes in the wealth of a
nation, or of the world, without any corresponding change in the quantity or quality of
the " goods." A general rise or fall of prices,
due to monetary causes, will thus produce a
shrinkage or an expansion of " wealth " which
has no substance. Though statists can make
corrections of such errors, the reliance upon
current prices as the measure of " wealth "
will continue to be a source of some confusion
in the study of wealth.

When stock is taken of the things which
constitute " wealth," the ordinary conception
of it will be found too materialistic. The
good-will of a business must rank as wealth,

just as much as its factory buildings : though immaterial, it is saleable. Sometimes it has been contended that the efficiency, skill and other qualities of business ability or labour power, should be reckoned in the national wealth. But this would be wrong. Under slavery the productive capacities of the slave are parts of the saleable commodity he is; but when persons are not wealth neither are the capacities that are inseparable from them. Only the particular services which they can render and hand over to a purchaser are wealth. Thus the skill or knowledge of a doctor is not wealth, but the operation he performs or the opinion which he gives upon a case is wealth. So it is with all sorts of professional and personal service. The cooking and the waiting are wealth in the same sense as the food which they prepare and serve : the lesson ranks as wealth on equal terms with the text-book. Where, however, personal skill or effort is applied to material goods so as to change their form or place, it is usual to consider this skill or effort as entering into the goods and so adding to their wealth. So wage-labour and work of management are not commonly accounted wealth, but are included in the wealth of the goods they help to produce. In reckoning wealth from the social standpoint it is clear that they cannot be counted both

ways, and it is far more convenient to count
them in the goods whose market value they
enhance.

If stock were taken at a particular moment
of the wealth of a man or of a nation, of
course only material forms would count, for
services involve a lapse of time. But
professional, domestic, recreative and other
services, which are not merely applied to the
production of material goods, must evidently
rank as separate sorts of wealth, if they are
sold. In any inventory of the wealth of a
nation taken over a period of time they must
be included. The part they play in the
general fund of wealth will be more evident
when we treat of " income."

The arrangements for producing or pro-
curing these various sorts of tangible or
intangible wealth we call the economic or
industrial system. The latter term it will be
more convenient to use. But it will require
a stretching of the term " industry," so as to
cover all those activities which go to make
any sort of wealth, including the services of
the judge, the clergyman, the acrobat, or
the trade-union secretary. So not only the
extractive industries of agriculture and mining,
the manufacturing, transport and distributive
trades concerned with material goods, but the
work of government, the learned professions,
the fine arts, all gainful recreations and amuse-

ments, must be brought under the "industrial system."

The product of all these forms of industry is wealth and its amount is estimated at its market prices.

There is, however, another broader and widely different use of the term wealth which identifies it with human welfare or well-being. " There is no wealth but life. Life, including all its powers of love, of joy and of admiration. That country is the richest which nourishes the greatest number of noble and happy human beings ; that man is richest who, having perfected the functions of his own life to the utmost, has also the widest helpful influence, both personal and by means of his possessions, over the lives of others."[1]

John Ruskin and some other prophets of this wider wealth have denied the validity and the utility of the narrower Political Economy. Mere statements about marketable goods, measured in terms of money, do not, they urge, afford any useful information as to the effects of their production and consumption upon human life and happiness. Other students of society have also questioned the validity of separating the study of economic processes from that of other social processes and making of them a " science " of industry.

This criticism, so far as it has point, is

[1] Ruskin, *Unto this Last.*

applicable to all scientific specialism. The whole world of phenomena is a unity of intimately connected parts, and every breaking off of any section for separate study is of necessity an act of mutilation. But such separate studies are essential to intellectual progress, and the mutilation is not fatal to their use, provided that it is kept in mind, and the subject of the special study is not treated as a completely rounded whole. The chief danger from such scientific specialism arises where the science is made into the basis of an art and maxims of human conduct are erected on it. The scientific study of industry may show that certain acts of individual or national policy make for an increase of marketable wealth. To convert this "is" into a "must," and to urge this discovery as a sufficient ground for individual or national conduct, without taking into due account other effects upon public welfare which may or must arise from this commercially profitable policy, is evidently unjustifiable. For when a person or a nation is considering what line of conduct to pursue, he must take into account at one and the same time all the probable advantages and disadvantages. In a word, he must take for his criterion of conduct the wider standard of wealth which identifies it with welfare. The advice which the mere economist may offer to the statesman must therefore always be adjusted or corrected by reference to this larger conception of the public good. An immediately or even a permanently profitable business policy may be negatived by considerations of wider utility.

But these admissions do not mean that either a science or an art of industrial wealth is invalid. On the contrary, both are essential to the progress of the wider science and the wider art of " politics " or social conduct. Not only do we need to learn, by separating the industrial from the other social phenomena for closer inspection, how the industrial system is made and works, but we also need to know what are likely to be the effects of proposed changes upon the working of this system and the quantity of marketable wealth it yields. Both sorts of knowledge are of service to citizens and statesmen. Neither is sufficient as a guide to conduct : both are but tributaries to the wider current of information that helps to mould the policy of the commonwealth.

CHAPTER II

To a young man first entering an occupation as an artisan, clerk, tradesman or professional man, the larger business world necessarily appears as a confused, intricate mass of vague forms and happenings, fragments of which float before his vision and his mind in the talk of his friends and neighbours, in the columns of the newspapers, in shop-windows and street life, and in the acts of retail purchase in which he spends his earnings. His single focus of clear vision is furnished by the definite regular work in which he is personally engaged. The unity of industry, the very notion of it as a system, long remains hidden from him, or is at best a vague generalization. But the reality, the structure and the working of the business establishment to which he is attached soon impress themselves clearly on his mind.

Though at first he may know intimately only the process in which he works and the other workers doing similar work near him, he soon picks up some knowledge of the other processes in his department, and, as he moves about and makes acquaintance with his fellows, he learns more of what goes on in other departments. If it is a manufacture, he sees the raw materials and the finished products, and, according to his intelligence and interest, gets to know something about the machinery and the skill used in the several stages of the manufacture. Gradually he will acquire a clear grasp of the business organization which underlies the manufacturing processes, the work of overseers and of the management, some comprehension of what goes on in the office where the clerks are registering all the doings of the factory. Even of the acts of buying and selling most remote from his personal part he may get some understanding, especially if he is organized in a trade union with his fellows and learns the ways in which buying and selling may affect his work and wages.

An intelligent operative thus builds for himself a pretty accurate image of the material structure and the personnel of the factory or workshop in which he is engaged. The premises, the buildings, the machinery and tools, the power, the raw materials and produce at various stages of manufacture, some money in the till and the bank, the various grades of employees and the management, will stand out as distinguishable features. The clerk in the factory office, the timekeeper, the manager, will see substantially the same picture, but, looking at it from a different angle of vision, they will see or realize some parts more clearly than others, and assign a different importance to the different parts. Disregarding human considerations and regarding the factory merely as an industrial instrument, it will be seen that the manager is in the best position to assess the relative importance of the various factors as cooperative parts in the business. This does not imply that the manager is more unbiassed or disinterested in his motives and his judgments than the workman. In both cases special interests will to some extent distort vision and valuation. The advantage of the manager is a technical one : he is in a better position than the process-worker to see the various parts of the business in their several sizes as contributory to the whole. For management, as we shall recognize, is the unifying, cohesive and adjusting factor in the business : the manager also alone knows the monetary " cost " which each involves, and has thus a common standard measure of importance which he can apply. For these reasons it is desirable that an operative or clerk, who seeks to get a most reliable image of the business, should try to supplement his wage-earning, point of view by seeking to assume that of the manager and to realize how the business looks from that situation.

The business, or smallest organized unit of industry, thus roughly visualized, would take some such shape as this

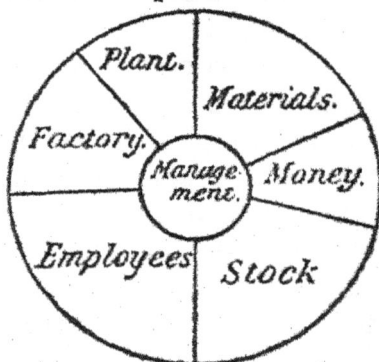

If instead of a factory, we took a mercantile establishment, a mine, a retail shop, a farm, though all the details would be different, the general structure would be found to be the same. Raw materials, stock, tools, premises, labour and management would all be there co-operating to a single industrial end, though in widely different proportions. In a commercial house, plant would play a much smaller part, there being little machinery or tools; materials and stock would be only a different arrangement of the same goods, and money would figure more prominently. In the farm, as in a mine, premises, including land, would of course bulk far more largely than in a factory. Again, many businesses are not tightly contained in single premises. A bricklayer, working for a firm of builders, will realize the business as consisting, not in a fixed yard and office, but rather in a number of changing jobs. A railwayman will have to bring a wide vision and imagination to realize the structure of his business.

Businesses belonging to the same trade will be found differing enormously in size and in structure. In farming at one end of the scale will stand the peasant working a small plot with his own hands for the subsistence of his family, at the other, some vast cattle ranche or some bonanza grain-farm worked by costly machinery. In goldmining you have the solitary placer or the gigantic Rand company. So in almost every species of industry, transport, manufacture or commerce. But in the handling of material wealth all the factors which we found in the factory will be present in some sort or size : there must always be some premises, tools, materials, stock, money, labour and management, though the last two may be performed by the same persons in the simplest businesses.[1]

[1] The private factors of production are conveniently grouped under four heads as Land or Nature, Labour, Ability, and Capital. The separateness of these four has often been challenged and is not always capable of logical defence. In particular, it has been urged that Land might be treated as a form of Capital, for most land that has

Even when applying, as we must, our wider conception of industry to the production of non-material goods, we find the same general outlines of the business structure applicable. Turning to the theatre, the doctor's or lawyer's " practice," the school, the hairdresser's, or any other organized arrangement for producing and selling " services," we shall find that though the material apparatus, premises, tools, etc., are sometimes reduced to very small dimensions in comparison with the factor of personal skill and energy, they are always there. Indeed, some of the service-producing businesses, such as a theatre or a

value is " improved," and the improvements incorporated with it are clearly capital. Moreover, for most purposes of finance and book-keeping, land values are included in capital. But in our concrete account of industry it is important to maintain the distinction. For in origin and Nature Land differs from every sort of capital, and an intelligible theory of payment for the use of the factors enforces the need for the distinction.

Concrete capital will consist, then, of (1) buildings and other fixtures, (2) machinery and tools, (3) materials and stock, (4) money. The two former are often called "fixed" capital, standing as they do fixed at some point in the industrial stream to assist in driving raw materials or goods towards their final destiny as producers' or consumers' commodities. The two latter, (3) and (4), are usually called "circulating" capital, for their industrial work keeps them moving from one place in the industrial system to another.

The separateness of the factors does not imply a separateness in their ownership. In most of the smaller or simpler types of business, the worker, or some of the workers, own also some of the capital or the land, and give out the ability required in conducting the business.

school, involve a very elaborate material
equipment which brings them under the most
advanced form of modern capitalist enterprise.

But in our endeavour to get a firm conception of a "business" as the unit of
industrial structure, we are not yet out of
the wood. It is clear that many of the factories, shops, etc., which we are taking into
consideration are not separate independent
businesses. They are only separate establishments. Though formerly it was very unusual
for several factories, mines, shops, to be owned
and managed by the same persons, it is quite
usual now in some branches of industry.

It is the unity of financial control that
gives unity to a business. All the mills
belonging to a single company must therefore strictly be regarded as making one
business, just as all the retail stores of Lipton's
or Wanamaker's make one business. Nor
need a single business in this sense consist
always of a number of mills or shops of the
same sort in various places. It may extend
its operations into several different trades,
as where a great departmental store has
attached to it a farm, a furniture removal
department and a carpet factory, or where
a railway owns and operates engineering
works and coal mines. Nor is this the only
way in which the plain outline of the single
business may be blurred. Many apparently

separately controlled establishments are in their finance or management, or both, dependent on some larger and stronger firm. Many shops in such trades as tobacco, jewellery, shoes, ironmongery, if not mere branches, are virtually agents selling on commission certain classes of articles belonging to particular manufacturers or furnishers. Other workshops, producing subsidiary articles or executing repairs, are often closely attached to and dependent upon some big manufacturing neighbour. Many subtle forms exist of such connections between what at first sight appear separate businesses. The question of financial and even of managerial independence is thus seen to be a matter of degree in many instances. But it is not necessary for our purpose to require the application of rigorous logic in such definitions. It will suffice to recognize that what binds together the different elements of a business, and gives it unity of structure and productive efficiency, is what is called the management. If a fair amount of discretion and substantial liberty in the conduct of the establishment is possessed by the manager, his mill or mine or shop may reasonably rank as a separate business for the purposes of a general description of the industrial system, although the supreme and ultimate decision may be vested in some body of shareholders.

We shall, then, treat the single complete establishment as a separate business for the purposes of our survey, except when it becomes necessary to give emphasis to capitalistic combination and control. The industrial system is thus first realized as an elaborate arrangement of business-cells grouped together by certain resemblances of form and purpose into Trades. Businesses making or handling the same sorts of goods are considered to belong to the same Trade, even though their methods of work may differ very widely. Watchmaking by hand is a very different sort of work from watchmaking by machinery, but since the products are in both cases watches, they are regarded as belonging to the same trade.

So with other work which is partly handwork, partly factory work. Not only the mode of work but the materials may differ. Houses may be built of stone, wood or brick, but they come under the general head of the building trade. Generally, however, a marked difference of material is held to denote a different trade. So the iron bedstead makers are a different trade from the wooden bedstead makers. The test is the Market. Businesses that compete effectively for the sale of their goods in the same Market are taken as belonging to the same trade. But here, too, no hard and fast line can be drawn.

Hand-made and machine-made watches certainly so compete : so do wooden and wax matches : these evidently belong to the same trade. But though wooden and steel furniture compete, their competition is less close and their markets not identical. Gas and electricity compete for lighting, and yet they must be classed as different trades. It is sometimes convenient to speak of the building trade, sometimes of the building trades. The woollen or the shoe trades break up into special trades, often on a local basis. Different grades or qualities of the same kind of goods sell in a different market, and are regarded by the makers and the buyers as different trades. Again, locality is a basis for distinguishing trades, especially when, as is common, it involves some difference in work or product. So the Clyde and the Tyne have their own ship-building trades, the South Wales coal trade stands apart from other English coal-mining, Leicester and Northampton have their own shoe trades. These illustrations will suffice to show that as much latitude exists in the ordinary use of the term Trade as in that of Business. But upon the whole it is best to consider the limits of a Trade as defined by those of a Market, and to regard businesses, whose products meet and compete fairly closely in the same Market, as members of the same Trade. A Market is defined to

be not any particular market place in which
things are bought and sold, but " the whole
of any region in which buyers and sellers are
in such free intercourse with one another that
the prices of the same goods tend to equality
easily and quickly."

Thus there is a world-market for Consols,
for gold, diamonds and a few important
durable goods and materials such as wheat
and wool ; for most others the national area
covers the market ; and in the case of very
bulky, perishable or immovable goods, a number of small local markets exist. Of course
inside each market there is room for some
differences of make and quality and reputation,
which affect the competition and the price.

But the main distinctions here suggested
need not prevent us from holding that businesses can be grouped into separate trades
according as they are engaging in supplying
goods to a common market. So the operative
in a spinning mill at Bolton, or a shoe factory
at Leicester, will soon extend his economic
vision from the particular establishment in
which he works to the groups of similar
establishments which constitute, first the
local, and then the national cotton or shoe
trade. The vaguer looser conception of an
international or world trade may come later
as a slight qualification of the narrower and
more practically valuable conception.

Of course the unity and solidarity of his trade will be seen to be much weaker than that of his business. At first it will appear as a number of separate and competing businesses. But among the local members of a trade some concerted action and some organization will usually be found. The employers in each trade are apt to meet in a society or federation to gain information and to safeguard and advance their interests relating to purchase of materials and labour, methods of production, markets, etc.   The workers in the same trade also join together for various economic and social purposes. A further development of trade structure consists in the formation of a machinery of agreements, conferences and conciliation boards for adjusting the interests of capital and labour in relation to wages and other conditions of employment.

The worker will thus come to set a definite meaning upon his Trade. In getting this knowledge he will gather a notion of how this trade stands in relation to some others.   He will perceive the very close dependence of his trade upon other trades which supply the materials on which he works and upon the trade or market which buys the product of his trade. If he is a shoe operative, he will find his trade especially affected by anything that happens to the tanning trade

which furnishes the leather, or to the merchants or retail shops which take from the
manufacturer the shoes. If he is a woollen
weaver, he will realize the close dependency
of his trade upon the conditions of the raw
wool trade on the one hand, the clothing
trade upon the other. For he will see important forces that affect his work and wages
issuing from either of these directions. If he
carries his inquiry and reflection further, he
will make the important discovery that the
trade in which he works is but a link in a
chain of industries engaged in converting
raw materials into finished goods and putting
them into the hands of consumers.

If he is a shoe operative he will see his
chain running thus—

Farmer......Tanner......Shoemaker......Shoe merchant......Shoe shops.

If he is an engineer they will run thus—

Mining......Smelting......Steel works......Machine shops.

But every trade will be found to have
some other trades linked directly with it and
working towards the production and supply
of the same articles. There will be some
branch of farming or mining engaged in
extracting raw materials from Nature. Then
will follow one or more manufacturing processes, and after that some wholesale and
retail distributive trade.

CHAPTER III

OUR shoe operative, weaver or other specialized worker, now looking out from his trade,
will realize it as a member of a series, all
bound together by common interest in forwarding the production of some particular
goods. Though he may know little about
other trades, he will rightly conclude that they,
too, similarly run in series of productive and
distributive processes. As a consumer buying various sorts of food, clothing and other
commodities, he will recognize that he is
tapping one end of a number of similarly
constructed industrial chains. So industry
will begin to widen out to his vision as a
number of series or streams of processes,
each series or stream engaged in the separate
task of forwarding some raw materials on
the road to consumers' goods. He will see,
not only the boots he wears, but the loaves,
shirts, tables, books, tobacco, and other
things he buys, as the ends and objects of
a special series of trades. But he will soon

observe that the separateness of the goods, loaves, boots, shirts, etc., gives an exaggerated notion of the separateness of the lines of trades through which they pass in the making. For he will recognize that there is no complete series of trades entirely devoted to making, moving and selling boots. The farmers who supply hides to the tanners, supply also carcases to butchers, grain to millers, and enter into other series of products. The tanner, too, furnishes leather to other manufacturers besides shoemakers. Many retail shops sell other articles besides shoes. The same will turn out to be true for any other series of trades. The streams of production merge or overlap at certain points. Certain early extractive and manufacturing processes will be found to figure in a great many of the series. Farmers, miners and others who get raw materials from Nature, must perform the opening process in all the great productive series. When their extractive work is done, the great variety of materials it affords is sorted and is put through a number of different processes. The later manufacturing processes are more numerous and more specialized, while the work of distributing and selling goods often brings together in the same trade or business a quantity of goods which in their manufacture belonged to different trades.

If, then, we take the symbol of a stream, and speak of currents of industry carrying raw materials past the different stages of production, until they flow over the retail counter into the hands of consumers, we shall find the stream issuing from a few sources, dividing into an increasing number of separate currents as it flows on in manufacture, and again gathering into comparatively few channels as it passes along the mercantile stages towards the consumer.

But the actual structure of industry is, of course, much more complicated than this picture would imply. Some of this complexity will appear comparatively early to our intelligent workman taking observations from his place in a factory, a mine, an office. He will recognize that all trades are not engaged directly in the work of pushing raw materials through the main stream of industry towards consumers' goods. The shoe operative will be aware that there are one or two trades we have not mentioned which are nearly as important in their bearing on shoe manufacture as the tanning trade itself, viz. the trades which supply the machinery and power used in his factory. This machinery and power are of course themselves the final products of a series of productive processes, converting raw materials into these forms of capital. They do not figure at the end of our industrial system as " consumers' goods." They find their goal in becoming " capital," and are used up, not as commodities, but as plant and other aids to production. In examining the structure of a business we recognized that premises and machinery as well as materials were needed. It is only the materials which are the objects of the process of manufacture and which flow down the stream towards consumers' goods. The buildings, machinery and other plant are used as means to this end. But they have to be produced, and their forms are gradually worn out in the work of assisting to make hides into leather, or leather into boots, or in some other useful work.

The shoe operative, then, will see that his main current of trades, converting cattle into shoes, must be reinforced by various tributary trades engaged in supplying the tools, power, buildings, etc., required at each stage in production.

Taking the single factor of machinery, he will correct his picture as on p. 34.

But there are other trades which he will see assisting to produce and maintain the buildings and other appliances of the factory, the light, heat and power required : these, too, he must fit into his fuller picture. Since it is evident that the farmer, tanner, merchants and retail shopkeepers, who stand in the direct stream of industry, likewise use plant, machines and other products to assist them in their work, it follows that at each process the main stream must be fed by tributary streams which flow, not to the ultimate consumer, but to some single stage in production, supplying new stores of auxiliary goods to producers.

Of course, if one likes, it is possible to regard

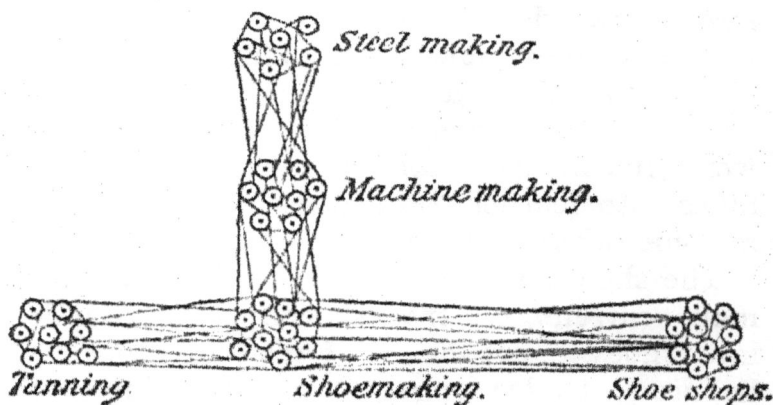

Steel making.

Machine making.

Tanning.   *Shoemaking.*   *Shoe shops.*

the machinery, buildings and other plant as being gradually worked up into the goods they assist to produce, and so flowing down the main stream to consumption. But this view need not concern us here.

Now these tributary trades, supplying the " fixed capital " to the main stream, are often larger and more important than the special trades they feed. For some of them supply with the same sorts of fixed capital not one but many trades in the main stream of industry. The iron, steel, engineering and machine-making trades are important tributaries at every point of the factory system. So are the building trades. The mining, the principal metal and building trades are chief supports of the permanent fabric of so many special trades, that they are often spoken of as " fundamental " industries. When anything serious happens to any of them, the effects are soon seen in every part of the industrial system.

But there are other bonds of common interest between the trades in the main stream of production besides these " fundamental " industries.

The same sort of raw material may be utilized either as a chief ingredient or as a subsidiary in many main branches of production. The chief grains, timber, textile fabrics, iron, coal, stone, clay, etc., form raw material in the making of many different commodities, and the different trades using any one of them are related by powerful bonds of sympathy and antipathy. Such is, for example, the relation of shoe-making to saddlery and upholstery (through leather), of jam-making to biscuits or to aerated waters (through sugar). Where such community in use of material exists, it breeds a sympathy between trades. For anything which improves or impairs the supply of their common material causes gain or injury to all. So far there is sympathy. But anything which gives one trade a better pull than others upon the supply injures these others. So far there is antagonism. Oil and rubber are instances of the recent growth of two ingredients of vital importance to many trades.

Some trades are in close enduring sympathy, because they supply important complementary ingredients to one or several important industries. The iron and coal trades furnish the most obvious example. But this sympathy is very strong in many special trades, as between the fruit-growing and sugar-refining trades, or wine-growing and bottle-making, or between the various trades furnishing materials to the building trades.

On the other hand, a keen antagonism is set up between certain trades by reason of the possibility of substitutes. When different materials can be used to supply the same wants this hostility exists. Wood and iron in many sorts of furniture or building; cotton, wool, linen in articles of clothing; tea, coffee, cocoa among drinks, will serve as instances. So electricity, gas, oil and steam compete against one another as sources of industrial, locomotive or domestic energy.

These trades, and others subsidiary to them, are thus brought into conflict, and anything which benefits one is apt to injure the others. The substitution may sometimes be in materials, sometimes in process, sometimes in final commodities; but wherever it operates it breeds opposition.

•Among what first appear as separate trades engaged in converting raw materials into commodities, we perceive, then, many connecting bonds of union and opposition. The series of industrial processes cross, fuse and separate at various points: no series runs a completely isolated course.

But there are two sorts of industry which deserve particular attention as unifying influences, viz. transport and finance. They are not fundamental like mining and agriculture, but pervasive and connective. Wherever any business is carried on, a constant conveyance of materials to the business, and of finished goods from the business, is involved: every act of buying and selling involves some act of conveyance. The group of trades concerned with such conveyance must, therefore, occupy a place of peculiar prominence in the industrial system. Taken as a whole, they form an apparatus corresponding to the vasomotor system in an animal organism. In one sense, indeed, all physical work is movement of matter, and much of it forms part and parcel of every business operation. But in modern industrial societies transport in its special sense, the conveyance of persons, goods and intelligence from one place to another, becomes a highly specialized and important work. The railway and the steamship find a place in almost every series of productive processes. They furnish the physical links that give efficiency and continuity to the whole movement. Any stoppage of a great railway or a great shipping service paralyses a whole industrial area : even the cutting of telegraph-wires confuses and retards the whole working of industry. As industry becomes more complex, materials and labour are drawn from more distant and more numerous places to take part in more delicate and complex processes of co-operation, and the commercial working of the system depends more and more upon rapid and reliable information about their movements. For this reason transport is found in every civilized country to play a larger and more imposing part in industry, absorbing an increasing proportion of capital and labour, and presenting the most critical problems of control. When, as is the case in many large countries, the railroad is the sole effective means of transport, it may wield a power over the life, prosperity and industry of the population which is

despotic unless the government intervenes.
Every improvement of transport facilitates,
every breakdown of transport damages, simultaneously, all the industries concerned with
the production of material wealth.

Equally pervasive and more authoritative in its general control over all modern
industry is finance. Under that term we
include all business connected with the
production, protection and conveyance of
mcney, or purchasing power, and with the
creation of and dealing in stocks, shares and
other negotiable securities. We saw that
our science is concerned entirely with things
that have a marketable value and with
processes each act of which involves a purchase. So it is obvious that the industries
concerned with the production and application of purchasing power are in their influence
as critical and as pervasive as the work of
physical transport. The familiar saying
" Money makes the world go round " is a
popular testimony to the importance attaching to the sort of business enterprises which
produce and regulate the supply of financial
power. The forces issuing from finance are
operative everywhere throughout the industrial order. A great banking crisis paralyses
all industrial activities as surely and even
more completely than a breakdown in the
railway system.

Thus, though we recognize a certain sort of independence and completeness in a business or in a trade, we also recognize a number of ways in which businesses and trades are related to and dependent on one another. The common use of some particular material or source of power, the substitution of one material for another, afford special bonds of amity or enmity between certain trades. A few farming, extractive and manufacturing trades stand as common starting-points for a great variety of later processes. The industries of transport and of finance present a general connective apparatus.

But, finally, it remains to be observed that there exists a more general sympathy and opposition between all trades, due to the fact that they draw the very breath of life from common sources. Fresh streams of capital and labour continually enter industry to maintain, invigorate and enlarge its structure and its vital energy. In its first emergence, as productive energy available for use, this fresh supply of capital and of labour power, the new crop of young labourers and of new savings, is, in a " free " country, at liberty to apply itself to any special sort of industry, and all trades must draw for their needs upon this common and constant supply. They have, therefore, a supreme common interest in the size, quality and reliability of this supply, and in the terms upon which it is procurable. So every cause affecting the volume, the fluidity and the efficiency of the new capital and labour in a community, will affect all the several trades. As we examine the working of the industrial system in more detail, we shall see that many barriers block or impede the free flow alike of labour and of capital. But so far as labour and capital have liberty to enter different trades, or to transfer themselves from one employment to another, they must be regarded as forming common funds of industrial energy pulsing through the whole framework of industry, as the blood courses through the various organs and cells of the body, giving organic unity to the entire system.

CHAPTER IV

HOW THE INDUSTRIAL SYSTEM WORKS

PART I

WE have now obtained a comprehensive picture of an industrial system in which many clusters of businesses are grouped into trades, while these trades are arranged in order by series to carry on the work of converting the raw materials and forces of Nature into commodities and services for the use of man. The diagram on p. 43 presents the main features of this picture.

The mechanism of industry, continually taking in fresh supplies of materials from Nature by means of the extractive processes, carries them through a series of manufacturing, transport and commercial processes which changes their shape, composition or place, until they finally are tumbled out of the retail " hopper " as consumers' goods.

At each stage in the process stand supplies of the factors of production, land, labour, fixed capital, ability, engaged in this regular work of forwarding production, and all these factors, as they are used up or worn out in their productive work, are replaced by new factors themselves composed of materials drawn from Nature and prepared by a series of productive processes for the place they are to occupy. So the industrial system has its many suckers in Nature, everywhere drawing out materials and forces to be worked up, partly into consumers' goods, partly into new instruments of production.

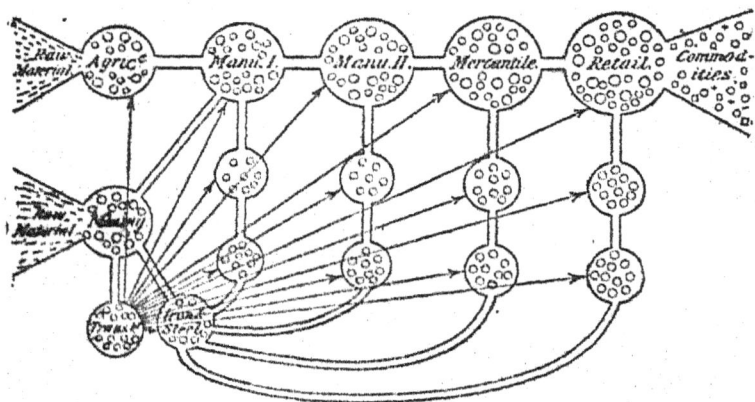

However intricate the system may be, there is nothing mysterious about its actual working. Every one knows, or can find out, how the chief kinds of materials, such as grains, fruits, animals, timber, textiles, coal, clay, metals, are worked up by different trades into the immense variety of finished articles which we use. The regular course of their productive career sometimes calls forth the image of a river, sometimes of a machine, sometimes of an organism. The organic metaphor is the

most useful, suggesting the likeness of industry
to the processes of taking in food, digesting
and assimilating it, converting it into working
energy and new tissue, and excreting the
waste. But none of these images is quite
correct. All suggest more regularity and more
smoothness of action than actually exist.
None of them takes proper account of one
essential fact, viz. that each productive act
done to the material in any process requires
the co-operation of a number of conscious
agents, the owners of the different factors of
production that are used. The bodily and
mental energy of countless little business
groups in a workshop or factory, a mine, a
railway station, a warehouse, must be got
into play over and over again to perform the
innumerable acts required to keep materials
moving down the industrial stream. These
acts are separate productive acts and they
require the application of separate stimuli.
How is the constant stimulation applied ?
Here again there is no mystery. Through
the industrial system there is a constant flow
of money which quite evidently performs the
work of calling forth the application of industrial energy from the owners of the different
factors of production. This flow of money
moves in the reverse direction to the flow of
materials and goods. The latter flow from
the extractive processes through the manu-

facturing and distributive processes until they pass over the retail counter.   The former enter the system chiefly at the retail counter and move up through the distributive, manufacturing and extractive processes in due course.

Take as an example the series of trades concerned with producing boots.

* The regular working of the boot trade requires that at each stage there shall be disposed a proper amount of factories and other fixtures, machinery and tools, employers and workmen, engaged in converting hides into boots and placing the boots in the possession of wearers.   All this apparatus is kept in being and in operation by a continual succession of payments of money made to the workers, employers, capitalists, landowners at the several stages of production.   These payments for the factors of production constitute wages, profits, interest, rent.   Whence do they come and how are they paid ?   A practical answer to these questions is given by posting oneself at the counter of a ready money shoe store doing a regular business with a turn-over of, say, £100 per week.   Customers buy and take away shoes, paying for them in cash. What does the shopkeeper do with the £100 he thus receives ?   Out of it he pays the weekly wages of his employees, sets aside something towards the quarter's rent and towards the interest on his borrowed capital, replenishes

his stock, and keeps what remains as wages of management or profits. All these payments are necessary stimuli to the retail process in the shoe series. They induce the owner of some factor of production to apply it in a new productive act which helps to maintain the supply of shoes intact in the retail store. The £100 we see is partly used to pay wages, interest, profit, rent in the retail business. These costs of retailing do not, however, take more than, say, £20 out of his £100. The £80 is handed on to the wholesale merchant, in an "order" for more shoes to replace in the retail store those which have been sold. The merchant who receives this £80, in his turn, applies part of it to pay the wages, rent, interest and profits in his office and warehouse, the rest, say £60, he uses to buy shoes from the manufacturer to replace those he has sold to the retailer. Similarly the manufacturer pays out of his £60 his current costs of production, say £30 in wages, rent, interest and profit, laying out the other £30 in a new purchase of hides and other materials. The tanner receiving £30 from the manufacturer will make a similar apportionment of the money at his stage of production, paying the farmer £15 for some fresh hides, which sum the farmer in his turn will use up in the payments he is called upon to make for raising cattle.

Here is the process we describe—

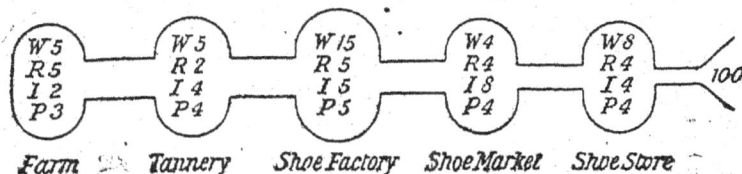

W5	W5	W15	W4	W8	
R5	R2	R5	R4	R4	100
I2	I4	I5	I8	I4	
P3	P4	P5	P4	P4	

Farm　　*Tannery*　*Shoe Factory*　*Shoe Market*　*Shoe Store*

It matters not whether the proportion given here for the distribution of the £100 spent on shoes corresponds to any known condition of the trades. What is certain is that the £100 paid over the retail counter circulates through the connected series of trades in the way described, that each payment out of it directly evokes a new productive activity, and that this is the means by which the industrial system is kept working. The prices paid in demand for finished goods are broken up and circulate through the productive processes, so as to maintain at each stage the activities required to keep up the supply.

If for boots we substitute loaves, shirts, books, bicycles, or any other article, the same analysis applies. The retail prices paid for the finished articles break up into a number of payments made at the different stages of production.

It will no doubt occur to some that trade, even under ordinary conditions, does not work in quite this simple, regular fashion. The credit system, for instance, does not always oblige a shopkeeper or a merchant to wait for cash from the customer in order to pay his way. The manufacturer, again, does not always wait for the merchant to order goods and to accompany the order by payment. He often produces in advance, and himself tries to stimulate demand.

But these niceties of actual commerce may be ignored in a presentation of the fundamental facts. It is evidently correct to say that in the regular working of the industrial system money enters as the universal stimulus through demand for commodities. Such demand visibly acts as the " demand " for labour, capital, land, ability, in each of the several processes.

The simplicity of our illustration requires, however, one qualification. Our picture of the industrial system showed that at each stage a tributary set of processes was engaged in furnishing the buildings, machinery and other fixed capital. It is evident that the " wear and tear " of this capital must also be provided for out of the only course available, viz. the retail payments for commodities. When, therefore, we assign at the retail stage £20, out of the £100, as costs, a part of which is to be paid to Capital, that payment must include depreciation or provision against wear and tear. Similarly with the payment made for capital in the warehouse, the factory, the tannery, the farm. Whenever fixed capital is used, some addition must be made to the payment so as to stimulate those tributary trades required to reproduce the buildings, machinery and other plant which are continually being worn out.

If, then, we apply to the economic system as a whole the working model furnished by the series of trades engaged in making and selling shoes, we seem to have a clear picture of it both as an industrial and a financial system. The constant regular flow of all sorts of raw materials through the various extractive, manufacturing, distributive processes, each furnished with a proper quantity of the different factors of production organized in businesses and trades, gives the industrial aspect. Its financial counterpart is a corresponding flow in the reverse direction of money, put in at the retail end, and working its way up the stream, stimulating, as it passes, each factor of industry so as to evoke a fresh activity.

PART II

This picture of the circulation of goods and money appears to give equal prominence to the two. To do this, however, would be unduly to exalt the part played by money in the industrial system. Though to the business man considering his investments and his profits, money often figures as the end and object of his activity, this is not actually the case.

Important as money is, it is a means and not an end. A means to what ? A means to the distribution of industrial energy on the one hand, and of industrial products on the other. As it circulates about the system, it is seen bringing labour, land, capital, ability, in different sorts and sizes, to the places where they are wanted, and apportioning the product among the owners of these factors. Since production is admittedly a means to consumption, the distribution of the industrial product must be accounted the primary object for which money is used. We have seen how money orders and stimulates industry in its various stages. It remains to recognize that this stimulation really takes shape through a distribution of the product. Money itself has no power to stimulate industry. Though habit makes money seem an end, a thing desirable on its own account, this of course is an illusion. The labourer wants not money but money's worth. So does the capitalist in seeking the payment of his interest, and the landlord in the payment of his rent. The actual work, then, upon which Money is engaged, as the retail payments dissolve and circulate through the system, is the distribution of the varied products of industry.

In the particular series of processes which end in the sale of boots, the sole product consists of boots, and if a primitive distribution prevailed, the wages, rent, interest and profits along the whole line would be paid in boots, which each recipient would have to wear, or to " swop " against bread, shirts, or some other goods paid in similar fashion as wages, rent, etc., in some other line of production. Then, at the close of an intolerable series of acts of barter, the shoe operative might get as the product of his labour, not shoes, but various other commodities, which are what he wants. Money was invented to save the risks and trouble of such barter, and to enable every special sort of worker to be paid in general wealth. For the money-wage he receives is nothing else than a general order upon the product, not of this or that set of trades, but of the whole industrial system. The tendency of civilization is to confine each worker ever more closely to a single narrow sort of work, a bit of a single process in one trade : the money-wage he gets reverses the process, putting him in possession of a bit of the product of every other trade. So, though he is only a laster or a finisher in his own trade, he is likewise miller, baker, spinner, weaver, carpenter, etc., through his capacity to get a share of the product of each of these other trades.

As a producer he is specialized, as a consumer he is generalized. It will be well to realize clearly how this transformation of special worker into general consumer is brought

about. How is it that a worker in a shoe
factory, whose work may consist in nothing
else than stamping leather, can change his
services into loaves, shirts, chairs, tobacco,
etc. ? His particular work is worthless taken
by itself; stamped leather is of no use to any
one. Only when the stamped leather has
passed through various other processes, and,
being made up into shoes, has been sold to a
customer, is the utility of his work realized.
Then out of the money-payment, which
measures the social utility of the whole set of
shoe-making processes, he gets his share.
Clicking, lasting or finishing has thus been
converted into money by means of the sale
of shoes. The clicker, laster or finisher, can
now take pieces of this money, and going
himself to one retail shop after another, can
convert it into the loaves, shirts, tobacco, etc.,
that he wants. As he buys loaves at the
baker's he sets a money stimulus at work along
the line of processes which go to make bread :
the baker and his assistants, the miller and his
men, the farmer and his labourers, get each
a bit of the money our shoe operative has paid
for loaves, and each of them with it buys at
the retail shops the various articles he needs.
Among these articles are shoes. So, some of
the very money which, paid over the shoe-
counter, passes to the shoe operative in wages,
is the money with which the shoe operative

himself bought loaves. The shoe operative needs bread, the baker and miller need shoes. We see how money, the price of shop-goods, enables each to supply his needs by exchange with the other.

Let us, however, set out this process of exchange a little more fully. Take the representative needs of man, say, loaves, boots, shirts, coats, chairs, meat, sugar, milk, books, crockery. Apply to each of these our image of a stream of production, each product having a separate series of four processes engaged in producing it. Suppose these to be the only economic wants, and that each man in the community wants the same amount of each. For convenience, substitute A, B, C, D, etc., for these ten products. The producers of A will then spend one-tenth of their pay in buying A, the commodities which they help to produce, one-tenth in buying B and one-tenth in buying C, and so with each of the other seven products. Similarly, the producers of B, C, or one of the other sorts of goods, will spend his pay, each using one-tenth to buy the finished products of the series of processes in which he works, the other nine-tenths to buy equal amounts of each of the other products.

It matters not where any man happens to be working, at A^3, B^4 or D, he will take his pay, and apply one-tenth of it at each of the retail stages, A^1, B^1, C^1, D^1, etc., so using an equal proportion of it to stimulate each series of trades. In this way the general product of the industrial system would be seen to be distributed in its entirety among all the different groups of special producers. The means by which this distribution was accomplished would be the money paid at each stage of production out of the retail prices of the finished products.

A^4	A^3	A^2	A^1	A
B^4	B^3	B^2	B^1	B
C^4	C^3	C^2	C^1	C
D^4	D^3	D^2	D^1	D
E^4	E^3	E^2	E^1	E
F^4	F^3	F^2	F^1	F
G^4	G^3	G^2	G^1	G
H^4	H^3	H^2	H^1	H
I^4	I^3	I^2	I^1	I
K^4	K^3	K^2	K^1	K

Though the actual process of exchange and distribution is, of course, far more complex, this is a true account of its essential character. Every man exchanges portions of his special product for the special products of every other man. So we see how the needs and actions of the consumer, expressed through money, form a perpetual bond of union between all the industrial processes. The industrial system thus exists primarily as a great co-operative

society of consumers.   For it is the pecuniary
stimuli proceeding from consumers that are
seen to maintain the industrial structure at
each point and to stimulate its regular activity.

This industrial apparatus, thus depicted,
seems to resemble an elaborate automatic
machine for the supply of chocolate and
matches.   Put a penny in the slot, you receive
an article and its removal causes each other
article, placed at a greater or less distance
from the outlet, to move one step nearer.   So
in our machine the money paid over the retail
counter stimulates a movement, first along the
main line of processes, then down the tributary
trades engaged in feeding this branch of production.   Its secondary effect, the spending
of the income received by each class of
producer, which applies a stimulus at each
other retail trade, seems equally automatic.

Thus we get an image of a fixed system of
industry, grinding out products and distributing them with mechanical exactitude.   Every
owner of a factor of production, worker, landlord, capitalist, employer, receives a portion
of the price of the final product his factor helps
to make, the money accurately furnishing the
stimulus necessary to maintain his factor of
production and to evoke a new productive
act.   The whole product, constituting the
" real income " of the industrial community,
would be distributed among the owners of the

factors, according to some law of mechanical necessity, just as the energy generated by a dynamo is applied at each point in the factory where it is wanted, in amounts accurately adjusted to the " work " there to be done.

The " real income " of every man, *i. e.* the amount of general commodities which he got, and his " money income," *i. e.* the money payment received for the use of his labour power, capital, land or ability, would be just what they must be to enable his factor to function. There would be no problem of distribution. The real income of the community would consist entirely of the aggregate of finished goods and services which regularly came out of the industrial machine.

Such an account differs in two important ways from the actual system of modern industry. It assumes complete fixity of industrial structure, and it assumes that the product of industry leaves no surplus over what is required to maintain the system and evoke its regular activity. Now both these assumptions are false. The industrial system is no rigid mechanism. Its structure, composition and working are not fixed. Its constituent trades and businesses grow and decay or change their character. The quantity and the sorts of plant and labour and other factors alter with changes of industrial technique or of business organization, and such changes are

always taking place. Within the last generation, the supersession of hand-work by machine-
work in the manufacture of shoes has completely transformed the structure of that trade.
In every industry and every country similar
changes are always taking place at a slower or
a faster pace. In an age of industrial progress
we must above all things study the laws of
industrial growth, how a business or a trade
increases its size and improves its structure
and its working.

Equally false is the second supposition, viz.
that the product of industry only just suffices
to supply the necessary stimuli to keep the
system working. When the boots, loaves,
shirts, and other final commodities turned
out of the various streams of industry, are
sold, the incomes paid for producing them are
not entirely absorbed in payments for the
various retail commodities.

Part of the money paid as rent, interest,
profit, wages is not applied, as we have hitherto
assumed, to demand consumers' goods. It is
applied not at the end of the various lines of
production, but at some interim point to cause
the creation of new forms of producers' capital.
In other words, it is saved, not spent.

So important is a clear apprehension of the
terms " saving " and " spending " that we
will here recall our outline diagram of industry.
If the working of this system were such that

the quantity of consumers' goods it could turn
out at E only just sufficed to supply the needs
of the various owners of instruments of production at A, B, C, D and E, and at the
different points in the tributary streams a^1, b^1,
c^1, etc., no growth of the system would be
possible. All the incomes, or money payments, made at the various stages, would be
regularly taken to E to be spent in consumers'
goods. But, if the system were able to turn

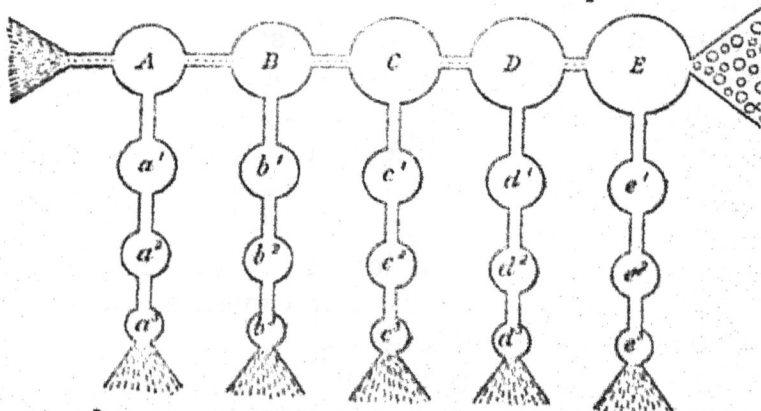

out a larger quantity of consumers' goods than
were required for the bare satisfaction of these
needs, it would be possible to apply some part
of the apparatus, not to the production of
consumers' goods, but to the production of
more plant and other fixed capital and to
getting with this increased machinery of
production larger amounts of raw materials
and power. Though the *ultimate* object of
such a proceeding is, of course, to cause more

consumers' goods to be procured, the *immediate* effect is to cause less consumers' goods to be produced. In other words, some of the money paid as income to the owners of capital, land, labour, ability, instead of being applied to demand more consumers' goods at E, is applied at, say, a^1 or c^1. So, instead of money payments circulating, as we have shown, from E through the direct line of productive processes from E to A and down all the tributaries, this money is applied at a^1, a^2, a^3, or c^1, c^2, c^3, as a special stimulus to the creation of more plant to be established at A and C.

This is the true industrial meaning of Saving, the spending of money income, not in buying consumers' goods, but in buying producers' goods; not in stimulating production along the main line of production of consumables, but in stimulating a series of productive trades engaged in making plant or other forms of capital at some particular stage. This abstaining from the purchase of consumers' goods, in order to buy more plant and other producers' goods, is evidently the only means of effecting the growth and improvement of the material system of industry. Here again money is seen as the directing force. The saving or the spending of £1 causes directly the same stimulus to industry and to employment of the factors of production, but the stimulus is applied at different points of the industrial system and has a different effect. In the case of spending it acts directly down a series of main processes of production, evoking energy to produce consumers' goods which are taken out of the industrial system to be consumed. In the case of saving it acts directly down a side channel of producers' processes, evoking energy to produce more capital goods, which are not taken out of the system but remain there as instruments of further increase of production. To the ordinary business man saving, at first sight, seems a merely negative industrial act, *i. e.* not spending, and putting the not-spent money in a bank. But actually it is as positive an industrial act as spending. Indeed, as we see, it is spent, but in paying people to make more capital goods instead of paying them to make more consumers' goods.

This is what spending and saving of income mean from the standpoint of the industrial organism and society. Of course it is true that an individual may save in another way, viz. by lending his " savings " to another person to spend them. A great deal of " savings " passes in this way into the hands of spendthrift individuals or bogus company promoters and other business sharpers, who spend the money which " saving " persons thus fail to save. Such false saving adds nothing to industrial capital, it simply means that one set of persons buys consumers' goods instead of another. The "paper savings" thus effected are devoid of industrial substance.

True saving, however, is the means by which the industrial system, on its capital side, grows. It always implies that certain individuals, instead of applying some part of their money income in stimulating production, by purchasing retail consumptive goods, apply it in stimulating production by purchasing capital goods in addition to those which hitherto sufficed to maintain the current of production. Some hoarding of consumable goods may be classed under saving, but in a general sketch of the working of industry it may be disregarded. The usual result of saving is to increase the quantity or improve the productive quality of the industrial system, thus enabling it to produce an increased volume of goods in a given time, provided that a sufficient rise in the rate of future consumption maintains the activity of the increased plant.

Turning once more to our industrial system as a mechanism for producing ten sorts of commodities—loaves, boots, shirts, etc.; and distributing them so that one-tenth of each sort passes to each of the ten classes of producers, we must revise our picture. If provision is to be made for the industrial growth of such a society, we must suppose that the quantity of loaves, boots, etc., which such a system could turn out, is in excess of what is needed by its members, or at any rate by some of them, and that some of the industrial energy which might have gone to making loaves, boots, etc., is able to be diverted into making improved machinery for flour mills and boot factories, or into producing new sorts of plant for making sorts of goods not included in the ten accepted lines of necessaries. This division of industrial energy is caused by the process which we call saving, or the application of purchasing power at points of the industrial system other than the retail shop. As the application of money stimulates not only capital but the other factors, so " saving " not only causes more plant, machinery and other forms of capital to come into existence, but causes the other factors, including labour, to dispose themselves differently from what they would have done if there were no saving.

For as a demand for, or purchase of, consumable goods is seen to act as a demand for the employment of capital and labour all along the series of productive processes, so a demand for more productive capital, due to saving, acts as a demand for more employment of capital and labour in the machine-making and other plant-making industries.

In an industrial system, where progress by saving is thus attained, the real income is no longer measured merely by the quantity of products produced for consumption in a

given time. The new machinery and other
capital added during the year to that which
previously existed, also belongs to the income
of the year. If, therefore, we accept the sum
of £1,800,000,000 as measuring approximately
the year's money income of the British nation,
the " real " income corresponding to it will
consist partly of the goods and services which
during the year have been withdrawn for
consumption by consumers, partly of the
additions made during the year to the various
sorts of fixed and circulating capital. Whenever a money income has been received by any
one as payment for the use of his labour, land,
capital or ability, one of these two sorts of
product, or " real " income, has been produced
to correspond. For the receipt of such money
payment is nothing but a financial register
of some productive act performed either by
the recipient or by some productive instrument he owns. Whether this productive
act consists in altering the shape of some
sort of material, changing its place, or assisting
to get it into the hands of some one who
needs it, or whether it consists in rendering
some professional, official or personal service
which ranks as " wealth," all such acts contribute to the real income of the nation, *i. e.*
that sum of tangible or intangible goods which
have a market value and have been added
during the year to the total stock of wealth.

CHAPTER V

COSTS AND SURPLUS

THE product of industry, which constitutes the real income of a community, is, as we see, entirely distributed in payments to the owners of labour, land, capital and ability for the use of these factors. These payments made at the several stages of production are " expenses of production."

These payments, we recognize, must make provision in a stationary industrial system for the maintenance of the fabric of industry, *i. e.* the various factors in their existing size and efficiency. In a progressive industrial system, such as that with which we are familiar, they must in addition evoke an increase and an improvement of the fabric. In a stationary system the whole of the payments, which formed the money income of the owners of the factors, would be spent in buying commodities, the retail goods and services turned out by the different series of productive processes. These goods and services when bought would be withdrawn from the industrial system and consumed.

In a progressive system a part of the income of the owners of the factors would be applied not to buy commodities but to buy new plant and other forms of productive goods capital, which when bought would remain as a permanent addition to the structure of industry, representing an increased power of producing commodities.

But if the size and efficiency of the industrial system is to be increased, provision must be made not only for increased size and efficiency of capital but for some corresponding increase in labour and ability. Now this increase of labour and ability is procured by buying consumable goods which by their consumption promote economic efficiency in preference to buying those which do not, i. e. by what is called " productive " instead of " unproductive " expenditure. If saving persons furnish increased or improved machinery of production, the full advantage of their action can only be reaped on condition that the general expenditure upon commodities is such as to provide an increased quantity and an improved quality of labour and ability.

This does not imply that all expenditure on luxuries or upon comforts and amusements which do not make directly for economic

c

efficiency is absolutely wasteful and injurious. For there are other purposes of life besides the economic. But it does imply that the expenditure shall be such as to provide such increase and improvement of labour and ability as shall keep pace with the increase and improvement of the capital structure. (The increased application of land, the other factor, being procured by an application of new capital, *e. g.* by road-making, does not require separate recognition here.) In an advancing industrial community, then, the income will be applied in three ways. One part will go to costs of maintenance for the several factors, one to costs of increase, and a third to unproductive expenditure. Now each factor of production has its own costs of maintenance. First let us look at labour. The costs of maintenance mean provision of necessaries of life for the various grades of workers, with any further expenditure for keeping up the supply of labour at the existing level of efficiency. This is commonly known as a subsistence wage. It just suffices to enable and induce a worker to keep on working and to bring up a family large enough to supply another worker to take his place when he is done. For various grades and qualities of labour the amount of this subsistence, of course, will differ. There will be some difference for individual workers in every occupation, according with their particular physique and their circumstances. This provision may be regarded as a " wear and tear " fund, the minimum towards which wages were always supposed to tend according to " the iron law."

Where higher elements of skill or intelligence are involved in work, this bare subsistence may rise considerably higher than the mere maintenance of physical life, containing some provision for education, recreation and other forms of expenditure, so far as they are needed to maintain the existing fund of physical and mental energy. Managerial or professional ability may thus, even if we ignore the conventional part of a standard of comfort, require a relatively high salary as pay for bare subsistence.

To this subsistence wage of the human factors must be added a corresponding provision for capital and land. Here an important distinction comes out. The provision for maintenance of labour forms a part, usually the largest part, of Wages. But the payment for the maintenance of capital is not included under interest, nor the payment for maintenance of land under rent. The maintenance of capital is furnished by a depreciation fund applied to replacing worn-out or obsolete forms of plant, etc. Interest is an additional payment to owners of capital after this depreciation has been met. Similarly in the case of land, the provision for the replacement of productive powers taken out of the land is not rent : a tenant must engage to " keep up " the land and to pay rent as well. Economic rent, like interest, is a payment over and above the provision for maintenance of the factor of production.

The costs of maintenance of the industrial system consist, then, of (1) a number of subsistence wages and salaries for the various sorts of labour and ability, (2) a number of " wear and tear " funds for the upkeep of the various sorts of capital and land. These may be considered a first charge upon the industrial product. Unless adequate provision is made for all of them, the system is starved, its fabric is " let down " and its productive power reduced. Such starvation sometimes occurs, even in countries where upon the whole a high development of industry has been attained. Under a bad mode of tenancy farmers may let down the land. Under the pressure of shareholders for dividends a railway or an industrial company may not make a sufficient payment out of gross profits into the depreciation and insurance funds ; or a telephone or tramways business, about to pass under public ownership upon agreed terms, may fail to maintain its plant in full efficiency. Such incidents, however, are abnormal. In general the obvious self-interest of the controllers and managers of industry secures the payment of the costs of maintenance.

If the whole of the industrial product were absorbed in these costs of maintenance there could be no industrial progress. But if there remains some surplus, after this provision has been made, the whole or part of it may be applied to increasing the size or improving the quality of the industrial system. The payments made for this purpose may be called " costs of progress." They will consist of the minimum payments needed to call into industrial use the various sorts and quantities of additional labour, land, capital and ability needed for effective co-operation in the enlarged structure of industry. Each of these additions involves the application of an extra stimulus beyond that required to secure the mere maintenance of the existing factors. More or better labour power can only be obtained by the payment of a wage higher than the bare subsistence wage. This " wage of progressive efficiency " will operate in several ways to increase and improve the supply of labour in any trade to which it is applied, or in the industrial system as a whole. By the higher standard of life which it admits, it will evoke and maintain a better physique and morale among

the workers.   Better food, housing and clothing will improve the "home," raise the
standard of personal dignity and intelligence
for the worker, enable the seeds of higher
education to take root and to bear fruit in a
better use of money and leisure, and in the
development and satisfaction of higher wants.
All these improvements of the mind and body
of the worker have their economic significance
in the larger quantity or better quality of
labour power he is enabled and induced to
give out.   Perhaps the most important direct
result is the better care and education of the
children, giving them a more favourable
start in life and thus raising the efficiency of
the next generation. This "economy of
high wages" is, of course, attended by certain
wastes, due to individual defects of character
or bad customs, which impair the rate of
progress and efficiency. But the familiar
instance of a quick rise of wages resulting in
an increased expenditure on drink need not
be regarded as other than a passing and
exceptional effect.

Although in more civilized countries a
general rise of wages is not now attended by
an increase in the birth-rate, nevertheless,
by reducing the still high infant mortality,
by lengthening the effective working life,
and by securing that larger mobility of labour
which brings workers from all parts of the

world to the place where their work is most productive, it increases the quantity and efficiency of the supply of labour in a progressive industrial system. The amount of income needed to evoke and sustain the enlarged and improved supply will, of course, differ in different industries, countries and conditions of the arts of industry. But these varying wages of progressive efficiency are necessary " costs of progress." If the wages of any class of labour, or the salaries of any class of ability, are increased at a pace so rapid that the increase is not absorbed in higher efficiency, or even evokes a smaller or a worse output of energy, as sometimes happens, such payment comes under a different head, to which reference will be made lower down.

We have seen that the payment of interest is not required to maintain the existing fabric of actual capital.[1] The depreciation fund suffices for that. But if more or better plant, machinery, and other forms of capital are wanted, as they are in a progressive

---

[1] This does not, however, imply that the payment of such interest is illegitimate or inadvisable. It is both legitimate and advisable. For if payment of interest on existing capital were sought to be suspended, it is likely that the owners of the capital would cease to make provision against depreciation, using this fund instead for temporary payment of interest while the plant was being " let down."

society, some positive payment of interest is usually necessary. For though the time may come when a sufficient number of persons can be got to " save," and put new industrial capital into the system, on condition that when later on they want to spend what they have saved, they can do so, without requiring that interest shall be paid them in the meantime for the use of their capital, that time has not yet arrived. A sufficient quantity of new plant and other capital goods can only be got by paying individuals to save, instead of spending, some part of their incomes. The notion sometimes entertained that all interest is an unnecessary or a wrongful payment because the new plant and other forms of capital are " produced by labour," involves a double error. In the first place, labour does not by itself, unaided and unorganized, produce anything in modern industry; it is only one of several co-operating factors. In the second place, reflection shows that saving involves among a large proportion of savers an effort or sacrifice (sometimes called " abstinence," sometimes " waiting ") which is necessary to the creation and functioning of new capital. This effort or sacrifice, like other productive services, must be bought and paid for. The necessary payment is interest. Though some saving would be done were no interest obtainable, the full amount of new capital needed and its apportionment among the several industries cannot be procured in a competitive industrial society without interest.[1]

The payment, then, of the minimum interest needed to evoke the saving that shall supply fresh capital to feed the growing industrial system, is a necessary cost of progress. While the wear and tear fund for the maintenance of capital will, of course, vary in amount for different sorts of plant, buildings, etc., it might appear at first sight that the rate of interest required to evoke £100 worth of new capital would be the same whatever concrete shape the new capital might take. And this is actually the case so far as fluidity of capital and freedom of investment exist. It is open to every saving person to put his savings into a new foreign loan, into Canadian rails, or into any of the countless new industrial stocks quoted on the Stock Exchange. He is thus helping to build warships, or to make locomotives, or to furnish machinery and other plant to some new capitalist enterprise. The real rate of interest which he will be paid for this service will tend to be the same whatever investment

[1] A Socialistic society,. were such otherwise feasible, though it too must practise abstinence and "save" for any increase in its capital, need not pay interest to any one. It will pay "real interest" to itself in the gains accruing from its enlarged fund of public capital.

C 2

he selects. This uniformity is concealed by the fact that what is called "interest" commonly includes an element of insurance against risk which is not true interest. If allowance is made for this payment for risk, which differs very widely with different investments, the actual rate of interest, or payment for use of capital, will be found to be fairly uniform over those fields of industry open to all saving persons for free investment. With the growth of modern methods of finance, especially the spread of joint-stock enterprise, an increasing proportion of the industrial structure comes under this uniformity of interest. An English doctor, or shopkeeper, or skilled artisan, who has saved a couple of hundred pounds, can apply his savings to lay down rails in Alberta, to set up a motor plant in Birmingham, to sink a shaft in the Transvaal, or to furnish electric light to some city in Argentina, and, allowance being made for difference of risk, he will get his £3, or so, for each £100 worth of saving that he does. This minimum interest will, of course, rise or fall somewhat according to the quantity of fresh capital required and the amount of surplus wealth available for saving. But at any given time there is a rate of interest which is just enough to evoke the required flow of new capital into these open fields of enterprise.

But it must be borne in mind that a large proportion of the business world does not lie exposed to the free flow of new capital. Large numbers of small or middling-sized businesses all over the world are furnished with the capital they need by the private savings of business men, supplemented by family or local borrowing. Thus in addition to a World Market for capital we have myriads of little detached local markets. In these markets there will be various special rates of interest, corresponding to the special rates of wages in the various labour markets.

A rise of interest, like a rise of wages, will operate in two ways to evoke a larger or better supply of productive power. It will, in the first place, stimulate the owners of existing plant and other capital to make a fuller use of it. Machinery will be speeded up ; where possible, double shifts will be put in ; reserve machinery will be brought into use ; credit will be stretched to its fullest forms, and every other economy of capital will be practised. In the second place, it will evoke more saving, causing some persons to curtail their spending, in order to get the higher payment offered for new savings.

What now of Land ? We have seen that out of the product a provision must be made for the " upkeep " of land, but that this " cost of maintenance " is not rent.   In a growing industrial system more use of land will be required to co-operate with the larger quantity of labour and capital.   The land already employed must be cultivated more intensely or otherwise put to better use, or else land not hitherto used at all must be brought into requisition.   Both these processes involve expenditure.   In order to bring into use more land, roads must be made, land must be cleared, drained, fenced and otherwise equipped for use. If land already in use is to be cultivated more intensely, more expenditure of capital in so cultivating it is incurred, and a larger provision may be required to meet the more rapid exhaustion of the soil.   In both cases, however, the " cost " involved is a capital expenditure.   It is not rent.   So far as maintenance and improvements are concerned land is capital.   The payment called Rent belongs to a different category.

We are now in a position to make a preliminary reckoning of the payments or provisions to be made out of the annual product for maintenance and growth of the industrial system.   First, there are the costs of maintenance, or wear and tear fund, for the different factors of production.

Secondly, there are the costs of growth, operating in two ways: (1) by evoking a better or intenser use of the labour, land, capital or ability already in use, (2) by calling into use new supplies of these factors.

If the whole product were compelled by some necessary law of Nature to apportion itself among these several uses so accurately that it was wholly absorbed in these costs of maintenance and growth, we should have a completely rational and socially satisfactory system of production and distribution of Wealth.

So far as mere maintenance and its " costs of production " are concerned, powerful laws of necessity do compel a fairly full and accurate provision. For though workers in a trade may be " sweated," in the sense that they are not paid a true subsistence wage, this can only occur where either these workers are subsidized from some other source, or where this worn-out labour power can be replaced out of a reserve of " waiting " or unemployed labour kept alive out of some public or private charity. Apart from these abnormal circumstances (a consideration of which will be found in Ch. VII.) " sweating " does not pay, and a trade habitually practising it cannot live. The case is even clearer as regards the costs of maintenance of capital and land. A failure to make regular and adequate provision against wear and tear means nothing else than the starvation of the business. Individual unsuccessful busi-

nesses suffer this starvation, but trades do
not thus perish, unless some change in the
needs or tastes of consumers render them no
longer useful. A provision which may be
regarded as almost automatic is thus made
for the maintenance of the industrial fabric.

But as regards costs of growth there is
no such security for adequate provision. The
surplus of wealth remaining after costs of
maintenance are defrayed does not automatically distribute itself among the owners
of the several factors of production in such
proportions as to stimulate the new productive energies required to promote the
maximum growth of production. Instead
of disposing itself in these proper proportions,
the surplus may be so divided as to furnish
excessive stimuli to some factors and defective stimuli to others, thus retarding that
full progress of industry which requires a
proportionate growth of all the factors.

In other words, portions of the " Surplus "
may be wasted, or, what is the same thing,
employed " unproductively." Whenever any
owner of a factor of production receives a
payment for its use in excess of what is
needed to evoke its full use he receives " unproductive surplus." The simplest instance
is the rent of land. We have seen that rent
is neither a cost of maintenance nor a cost
of growth. Its payment does not affect the

supply of land available for use in an industrial society. It is, of course, true that where private property in land exists, the payment of various rents may be necessary in the sense that the landowners may succeed in demanding them as a condition of giving the use of their land. But they are not necessary in the sense in which costs of maintenance or costs of growth are necessary, *i. e.* as payments for some voluntary effort or sacrifice. Their payment evokes no productive power. A general rise of rent does not bring into use an increased supply of land nor does a fall of rent put land out of use. (A rise of rent for a particular use of land, *e. g.* wheat growing, will, of course, increase the supply for that use, but by diverting some land from other uses.) If a landowner can get a high rent he takes it, if he can only get a low rent he takes that : so long as he can get some rent, however little, he will not refuse the use of his land. He will, of course, apply his land to that use for which he can get most rent. So long, therefore, as land remains in private ownership, it may be contended that, in order to induce owners to choose the use for their land which is most productive, they must be paid some trifling premium. To this extent only can rent be deemed necessary in the sense in which wages or interest are necessary.

The same is true, however, of any payment of interest in excess of the minimum, say 3 per cent. required to evoke the quantity of saving needed for the growth of the industrial system. If capitalists, willing to apply capital at 3 per cent. receive 6 per cent., the extra 3 per cent. stands precisely on the same level with rent. It is unproductive surplus, stimulating and supporting no useful effort. It is taken because it can be got; if it could not be got the capital would be supplied just the same. The same is true of any element of salary or of wages in excess of the needs of progressive efficiency for ability or labour.

Any payment to a factor of production in excess of the costs of maintenance and progress thus ranks as unproductive surplus. It is a source of industrial waste and damage in three ways. First, it furnishes no stimulus to production   Secondly, it takes away a portion of the income, or annual wealth, which might have been productively applied, if it had passed to some other factor. Excessive payments to some factors involve deficient payments to others, and since industrial progress depends upon proportionate growth of all the factors, the receipt of unproductive surplus must be considered an obstacle to industrial progress. Finally, in its effect upon the factor to which it provides excessive payment, it not merely does not promote

activity, it depresses it. For as the receipt
of rent, or excessive interest or any other
form of unproductive surplus, enables the
recipient to satisfy his wants without any
output of personal productive energy, it must
be held to have a negative influence upon
production, retarding the growth of industry.
It acts simply as a demand for idleness.

So far as the industrial system provides
for the regular distribution of the product
in payments which stimulate the factors to
maintain or to increase their output of productive energy, industrial health is secured,
and complete harmony prevails between the
several factors. As it is not to the advantage
of employers or capitalists to refuse to labour
such share of the product as is necessary to
sustain labourers and their families in the
level of efficiency needed to co-operate with
capital, so it is not to the advantage of labour
to beat down interest or profits below the
level needed to evoke the fullest use of capital
and managing ability. Not merely as regards
the maintenance fund, but as regards the
application of the productive surplus, there
is a harmony between the respective interests
of labour, capital and ability. Friction,
even violent conflicts, may sometimes arise
through the failure of one or both parties to
understand or to interpret correctly this
harmony of the three factors. Industrial

progress, doubtless, has often been retarded by endeavours of unenlightened employers, to beat down wages at the expense of the efficiency of labour, or of unenlightened workers to attempt to secure for labour higher wages or shorter hours or other improvements which the " profits " cannot bear. But so far as the industrial situation is clearly seen by all the parties concerned, there is a solidarity of interests in the proper apportionment of the costs of maintenance and the costs of surplus.

Discord arises over the emergence of " unproductive surplus." It is not to the interest either of the labour or the capital in any trade that a share of the product should be paid in rent. Both are *prima facie* gainers by a reduction of rent, even to extinction, though we shall see that both do not stand an equal chance of securing and holding the gain. The same is true of any other payment of unproductive surplus, *e. g.* abnormally high interests or salaries or fees. The only true bone of contention, the only valid cause of conflict between capital and labour, land, ability, is the unproductive surplus. It lies in the industrial system a source of continual disturbance, breeding economic maladies.

For this surplus of rents and other un-earned and unproductive elements of income represents a large and growing volume of industrial energy diverted from its socially useful purposes and put to positively noxious uses. A large part of this injury consists, as we have seen, in the mal-distribution of the product as between the claims of the several factors to a share. Rent or excessive profits to certain forms of capital imply that labour and other forms of capital are inadequately fed for purposes of industrial growth.

But there is another injury, sometimes even graver, which the taking of unproductive surplus causes. In our simple picture of the industrial system we have, in conformity with usage, left out of consideration one factor which plays an important part in modern industry, namely, the State. For though the State exists to perform other than merely economic functions, a large and a growing part of the work of government is concerned with the protection and promotion of industry. The defensive services of the army, navy and police, a large part of criminal and civil administration, are concerned with the protection of private property and of the economic activities of the people. Directly or indirectly, the public expenditure on sanitation, education and other services for improving the physique and morale of the people, must be considered as contributing to economic efficiency. Much legislation and administration, central and local, is industrial in its express intent, concerned with improving the conditions of labour, regulating the conduct of business and safeguarding the interests of the consumer.

So far as this work of the State contributes to the security and progress of industry, it is rightly regarded as a factor of production, co-operating with the labour, land, capital and ability of the individuals who engage in industry.   Although the State is not recognized as standing at each stage in the processes of industry, demanding its payment for work done, like the owners of the other factors, it is none the less true that the State must have its share.   It also needs its costs of maintenance, and of progress, to be paid out of the only ultimate source of all payments, the product of industry.   We shall concern ourselves later on with the methods by which the State comes to take her share. It is here sufficient to recognize that she takes it by the same natural or reasonable right by which the other factors of production take theirs, on the ground that she assists to produce it and cannot render this assistance properly unless she is paid her share.   For unless proper provision is made out of the industrial product for the upkeep and improvement of the State, defective public services may bring such insecurity and inefficiency as will stop the flow of capital and labour to the industries where they are needed, or prevent them co-operating effectively for the production of Wealth.

The reason why it has been necessary to make this passing reference to the economic work of the State is that without doing so the full measure of the waste and damages involved in the unproductive surplus would not be understood. For the surplus consists only in part of wealth diverted to owners of land and of favoured forms of capital and ability from other private factors of production. It consists in part also of wealth rightly regarded as belonging to the State, because it is needed for the efficient operation of the public services. When unproductive surplus forms a large proportion of the wealth that is distributed, it entails starvation alike of the other factors in the private industrial system and of the State.

Taking account, then, of the claims of the various factors of production, public as well as private, and of the scheme of distribution by which the industrial product is apportioned among the owners of these factors, we may thus summarize the result—

Maintenance (cost of subsistence)	A
Productive Surplus (cost of growth)	B
Unproductive Surplus (waste)	C

A. Maintenance includes (1) minimum wages necessary to support the various sorts of labour and ability required for the regular working of the industries in their present size and efficiency; (2) depreciation for wear and tear of plant and other fixed capital; (3) a wear and tear provision for land; (4) a provision for the upkeep of the public services which the State renders to industry.

B. The Productive Surplus includes (1) minimum wages of progressive efficiency, to evoke a larger quantity and better quality of labour and ability for the enlargement and improvement of the industrial system ; (2) such a minimum of interest as suffices to evoke the supply of new capital needed to co-operate with the enlarged and improved supply of labour ; (3) a provision for the improved size and efficiency of the public services rendered by the State to industry.

C. The Unproductive Surplus consists of (1) economic rents of land and of other natural resources ; (2) all interest in excess of the rate laid down in B; (3) all profits, salaries and other payments for ability or labour in excess of what would, under equal terms of competition, suffice to evoke the sufficient use of these factors.

CHAPTER VI

UNPRODUCTIVE SURPLUS

WE have seen that the actual process of distribution consists in the innumerable money payments made out of the prices of finished articles to the different workers, capitalists, landlords, managers, engaged in helping to produce the articles. Not only are the costs of maintenance thus paid out, but in the prices paid for the use of the labour, land capital, ability at each stage of production are included such elements of surplus, whether productive or unproductive, as the owners of these factors are able to get for themselves.

If, then, we deem it necessary to study the part played by the unproductive surplus, it is in the buying and selling of the factors of production that we must study it. We must examine the terms upon which wages, rent, interest and profits are obtained.

It will be most convenient to begin with the rents paid for the use of land. For rent evidently affords the plainest example of an unproductive surplus. As soon as thought began to be directed towards a science of wealth and industry, it was perceived that the rent of land differs from other payments in that the landowner undergoes no personal effort or sacrifice, and gives out no personal productive force in return for the payment he receives. The labourer gives the productive powers of his body for his wages, the employer gives his energy of mind and his time for his profits, even the capitalist postpones some present enjoyment in order to furnish the capital for which he is paid interest. The landlord alone takes his payment for doing nothing. He has not helped to make the land for the use of which he is paid rent. It is true that sometimes he helps to improve the land, making it more fertile or more accessible, by expending thought and capital upon it. But in such cases he gets a further remuneration which, though sometimes lumped along with rent, is not really rent. For rent, the price paid for the use of the natural properties of the soil, its fertility, its advantages of situation, is not a reward for anything the landowner has done, or an inducement for him to do anything, it is simply the price of certain services rendered by the bit of Nature which he has secured for his private property. If, therefore, we clear " rent " of other payments for improvement of the land, we see that economic rent is entirely an unearned, entirely an unproductive, surplus. Its rise and its fall have no effect upon the supply of land : the landowner simply takes as much or as little as he can get. That rent in this sense was a surplus, differing from the payments made to induce workers, capitalists and employers to apply their powers, was early and clearly recognized. To many early economists rent was the only surplus. Workers competed with one another for the sale of labour power until the wage they got was the lowest sum upon which they could subsist, or for which they would consent to work. Capitalists and employers competed with each other so that interest and profits tended to be cut down to a minimum. After these necessary " costs " of labour, capital and ability, had been defrayed out of the product, the remainder, the surplus, went to the landowner.

This was the doctrine widely accepted by many thinkers who were not at all concerned with the equity of the proceeding, and who drew no conclusion adverse to the rights of landowners to receive the rent. It is held to-day by many who base upon it an attack on private property in land, or the doctrine of " the Single Tax." So strong is their conviction that economic rent is the only surplus, the only unearned and unproductive element of income, that they attribute to the landlords the power to take in increasing rents the whole of the increase of Wealth produced by the modern arts of industry, beyond the bare costs of maintaining the necessary stores of capital and labour. To their mind rent is the unproductive surplus.

Now, if land were absolutely limited in supply and were a strict monopoly this view of rent would be substantially correct. The sole owner of an island would be able to take in rent all the product, not only of agriculture but of every other industry, over and above the wages of bare efficiency and other minimum costs of capital and ability. He could dictate his terms to the owners of the other factors, for he could refuse to each of them all use of land, without which their labour, capital or ability would be useless. There have been, and still are, landlords who possess in some localities this power almost intact. The squire who owns all the village with the surrounding country is able to impose on all the villagers the terms on which they shall work and live, fixing the rate of wages and the rents, the occupations, recreations, the religion and the politics of the inhabitants. If any one objects, he is at liberty to leave his native place and find work and a home elsewhere, if he can. The ground landlord in some towns has the same sort of power over many of his tenants. If he owns the whole town, or the whole of some district with special residential or commercial advantages, he can rackrent the shopkeeper, the doctor or the workman, whose trade, practice or employment compel him to live in that town or district. The extreme instance is that of the shopkeeper dependent upon local cus-·tomers. The landlord, on a renewal of the shop lease, can evidently raise the rent so as to take the whole or nearly the whole of the business gains attributable to the skill and industry of his tenant, or the increased profits due to the growing population and needs of the neighbourhood.

But though such extreme cases of land monopoly exist, they are the exception, not the rule. The power of landlordism is seldom unqualified. The supply of land available for any given use is seldom absolutely limited, and the whole available supply does not usually belong to one man. Although the Duke of Devonshire may own the whole of Eastbourne, he could not raise his ground rents above a certain level, for if he did many would-be residents and lodging-house keepers would decide to settle in Bournemouth or else-where, and tradesmen would follow. With cheapening transport of persons, goods and fuel, a manufacturer is less bound to a particu-lar locality than formerly, and the increased mobility enables him to get land for factories, warehouses, etc., on easier terms. The mere fact that a small number of men own all the best sites in a city does not give them the power of monopolists. Most men starting a business or seeking a house to live in are not bound to a particular estate, they can choose between the vacant sites or houses belonging to several landlords. Though London is still growing very fast, and all the land is private property, these facts have not prevented a large recent fall of rents in many residential neighbourhoods. A firm of printers, wishing to establish printing-works in the country, can buy or hire land at a little over the agricultural price. They can do so, because any landowner who should refuse them land upon such terms would know that they could go elsewhere and get it. The fact, then, that all the land of a city or a country may be owned by a comparatively few men does not enable rents to rise so as to absorb the whole industrial surplus.

Rent depends for its existence and amount not upon monopoly but on scarcity. For every sort of business some land is essential. Farmer, mining company, brewery, cotton factory, city warehouse, grocer, lawyer, must buy the use of some land. So rent must figure as an expense in every business. Every one, again, needs a bit of land for a residence, and so must pay a portion of his income as rent. Now it must be clearly understood that in each of these cases what is bought and paid for by rent is a particular sort or use of land. It is arable land, pasture, market-garden land, suburban ground, city site for a house, a shop, a warehouse, a profession, that is wanted. Now though every sort of business requires some land, it is quite evident that land plays a much more important part in some businesses than in others. In farming and mining it is a factor of paramount importance : in the professions and in some branches of wholesale trade or in finance it is a comparatively trivial factor. Now those businesses for which very little land is needed, and for which it is not a matter of the first importance just where that land lies, can evidently buy the use of land on easy terms. For their demand for land is small and the supply of available land for their purposes is large. They will thus be in a strong position to bargain with landlords, for they can make them compete with one another so as to beat down the price. On the other hand, those businesses which need much land or need land of a particular quality or position must pay dear for it, because their demand for the sort of land they want is large in proportion to the available supply of it. Farm rents in Ireland, before the time of Land Courts, were raised to an intolerable height, because the growing population in the land were compelled to seek a livelihood in the neighbourhood where they were born by bidding against one another for a strictly limited quantity of sufficiently fertile land. A mining company must usually come to terms with the owner, or one of a few competing owners, of a very restricted supply of coal or iron lands, its requirements for successful operation being large. We have already seen why the manufacturer not tied to a particular spot is able to get cheap land for a new factory while the local shopkeeper is liable to be rackrented on each renewal of his lease. The difference in the various cases is in the pressure of the scarcity of land. The fact that the quantity of land in England is limited, and the fact that the quantity of land within a convenient distance of the centre of each town is still more limited, do not give landlords the power to charge what they like for most uses to which land is put. Though the pressure of scarcity for certain purposes in certain places, e. g. for shops in Bond Street, for banking premises in the City, for allotments outside some towns or villages, may give landlords a tremendous pull, for many business or even residential purposes land can be got at what is held a " reasonable " rate, because the ⹁ effective supply of suitable land, though of course limited, is large in comparison with the demand. The fact that an insurance company, making enormous profits, wants a site for a new branch office, does not enable a landowner to charge a higher price than he could get from an ordinary shopkeeper or other business man for the premises. For if no special advantage attaches to the particular site, the insurance company has a large supply of competing land out of which to choose and need pay only the current market rate.

The price of land use, then, is determined directly not by its utility but by its scarcity, and that scarcity differs in different places and for different purposes. Land might have a high utility and yet obtain no rent. This is the case in a newly opened country with plenty of fertile and accessible land and a small population. Good land can then be had for the asking, or for some quite trifling sum per acre. The natural fertility does not enable its owner to extort a more than nominal price or rent, so long as there is plenty of it not yet taken up. Only when the farming population begins to press upon the fat lands, so that there is not any left, can a price or a rent be got. If in a fertile valley owned by several men there were room for twenty farms, equally well placed, and there were only nineteen settlers, the rent would be merely nominal, because the supply of land would be in excess of the demand, and each settler by making the several owners compete with one another could drive down the rent. But as soon as there were twenty-one settlers asking for farms the rents for all will rise up to a considerable sum per acre.[1] When there were nineteen settlers, land was in abundance, labour scarce ; with twenty-one settlers labour is abundant and land scarce. It is the coming in of scarcity which gives a price or rent to the land. As the scarcity increases, up goes the price of the land for sale or for hire. The fertility, the contribution Nature makes to the productive processes of agriculture, remains the same. The rise of rent is due entirely to the intenser scarcity, i. e. to the fact that more persons need the use of land.

Now most land, at any rate in a civilized country, is capable of being put to several alternative uses. Even as agricultural land it may be used for pasture, or for arable, or perhaps for fruit-growing. If it is near a town, it may have other possible uses, e. g. for market gardens or for suburban building sites. Now, if we take these different uses of land in the order in which they are here named—pasture, arable, fruit-growing, market

---

[1] In fact, up to a sum slightly higher than the least efficient or the poorest of the twenty-one settlers finds he can afford to pay.

garden, suburban site, it is evident that they represent a rising scale of rents. An acre of land available for all these uses would generally earn the lowest rent as pasture, the highest as suburban site ; the other uses fetching different rents between these extremes. Now why are pasture rents per acre lowest and suburban site rents highest ? Not because the use of land for a house or garden is intrinsically higher than its use for raising cattle. These varying scales of rental are not determined by utility but by the varying degrees of scarcity which they interpret and express. An acre of suburban land fetches a high rent because the number of available acres near the town is strictly limited, and the suburban population is growing. There is a scarcity of supply. An acre of pasture land fetches but a small rent, because there is commonly a large supply of remote land available for this use. Remove the scarcity of suburban land by some method of cheap quick transit which opens up large quantities of equally good residential land further out, down will go suburban site values. Prohibit the import of foreign cattle, up will go the rent of English pasture lands, which will now acquire a scarcity value. Though, then, it is the utility or service of land that is bought by rent, it is the scarcity of the different sorts

D

of land that determines the amount of the rent.

The growing needs of an increasing population in a country thus bestows a set of prices and rents for the different uses of the land, according to the scarcity of supply for the satisfaction of these different needs. So, taking the land as a whole, an average acre of pasture will fetch say 10s., an acre of wheat land say 20s., an acre of hop land say 30s., while brick land, market gardens, suburban lands will have their higher prices for an average acre. These may be regarded as the market prices for the use of land for different purposes. Of course there will be a great many of these market prices in different parts of the country. Each suburb, for instance, will have a price of its own at which, or thereabouts, good building land is for the time being procurable.

These local or other differences are all matters of the degree of scarcity, the pressure of the needs of the population on the supply of land.

The price of a particular use of land, e. g. for market gardening or for building, being thus determined, the different acres of actual land will of course fetch a higher or lower rent according to the amount of this use which they contain.

If scarcity gives a value of twenty shillings

per acre to ordinary wheat land, then wheat land which is better than the ordinary will, of course, get a proportionately higher rent, wheat land which is worse a proportionately lower.   And so it will be with the rent for every other use of land.   What is bought and paid for by rent is so much utility of land, whether for wheat-growing, fruit-growing, or site-use.   When one acre possesses a larger amount of this utility than another acre, of course its rent is higher, just as the weekly earnings of an efficient workman on piece wages are higher than those of an inefficient workman.

A lot of mystification has been imported into political economy by erecting into " a law of rent " these self-evident facts that a more productive acre fetches a higher rent than a less productive acre, and that if the least productive acre fetches no rent or but a nominal rent, an acre which is ten or twenty per cent. more productive will pay the whole of this superior productiveness in rent.

In point of fact there is no law of rent at all but only an application to the sale of land-uses of an arithmetical truism, equally applicable to the sale of everything.   You buy everything because it contains something useful that you want, and the more it contains of that " something useful " the more you pay for it.   If one acre of wheat land is twice as good for growing wheat as another you pay twice as much for it, if ten times as good you pay ten times as much.[1]

In the case of wheat land, what you buy is the ability of the land to produce a quantity of wheat in excess of the cost of cultivation. If that " surplus " or excess is a merely nominal amount, the price, or rent, paid is also merely nominal : if the surplus is large, the rent is proportionately large. When the necessary labour and capital for cultivating the land can be got at " cost " price, the price of the land-use, the rent, is equivalent to the entire surplus.

Put simply, this means that where labour and capital are abundant and land is scarce, the whole of the produce due to the co-operation of these factors is taken by the landlord. In other words, rent is the scarcity-price of land : it is the result of what has been called " the niggardliness of Nature," *i. e.* the fact that in many places and for many industrial purposes there is a shortness of supply of fertile or convenient land.

A considerable section of " the unpro-

---

[1] This does not, however, mean that an acre yielding 30 bushels gets a rent just twice as much as does an acre yielding 15 bushels. That would only be the case if wheat grew without human labour or capital. If 10 bushels pay the cost of labour and capital, then 5 remain as a " surplus " for rent, in the worse acre, and 20 in the better acre, which in that case is four times as good.

ductive surplus " passes as rent to landowners by reason of this scarcity.   But the belief that this element of surplus must always and everywhere grow, because Nature has set an absolute limit on the supply of land, is unwarranted.

The supply of land-use is not fixed.   The mere facts that nothing can be added to the surface of the globe, and that no considerable amount of land can be reclaimed from the sea, are immaterial.   For we are concerned with the quantity of land-uses available for economic purposes.   Now for these purposes the supply is not fixed.   Great Britain, for instance, does not depend for her land-supply upon her own small acreage.   For her industrial life, and her food, she has the world to draw upon.   And the world is expanding, so far as effective land supplies are concerned. Every new railway in Western Canada, every improvement in irrigation in Egypt or Australia, adds more land to the economic supply of Great Britain and of the world.   Moreover each improvement in the arts of cultivation, spreading as it does ever more rapidly over all civilized countries, though adding nothing to the area of cultivation, increases the quantity of productive energy got out of the land, which is just as good.   Modern science applied to agriculture is showing that enormous increases of yield can be obtained out of land, with no proportionate increase of labour.   This is equivalent to a large addition of new fertile land. So far as the interior resources of the land are concerned, the improved modes of discovering and working mines, so as to get out and obtain coal and metals, are adding enormously to our available supplies. If, again, we turn from the fertility and treasures of the land to the use of its surface for building and other occupations, we need not assume an indefinite and necessary increase of the scarcity which expresses itself in rising site-values. The spread of cheaper, quicker and more convenient transit adds enormously to the quantity of land available for these uses, and so reduces its scarcity value. The effect of a cheap electric train and motor service in reducing town rents will be considerable.

If the growth of population kept pace with these improvements, or if the population, though increasing more slowly, developed standards of consumption making greater calls upon the use of land for food, housing and other material uses, the scarcity of land would undoubtedly enable landlords to take in rent a larger share of the " surplus." So far, however, as the civilized world is concerned, the net tendency appears to be the other way, a dwindling rate of growth of population with an increasing quantity of available land. In Great Britain, though the growth of town life has led to a great increase of site-values, the total pull of land upon the surplus wealth has probably declined steadily during the last century; not indeed absolutely, but relatively. Though no close calculation is possible, it is tolerably certain that the wealth of Great Britain has grown considerably faster than the aggregate of rents.

If scarcity of land produces rent, scarcity of any other factor of production, capital, labour or ability, may be expected to yield a similar result. And so it does. There is only this difference. Since the landowner undergoes no effort or sacrifice requiring compensation, the whole of rent is scarcity value. But, as we saw, labour, ability and capital have to receive from the product their costs of maintenance and growth. It is only what they can sometimes get in excess of these that corresponds to rent. Wherever, however, one of these other factors can get into the position which landlords occupy when they draw rent, i. e. if they can make their factor scarce, they can get a similar surplus.

Because capitalists commonly compete with one another, it is sometimes supposed that the interest which they receive cannot contain a " surplus " or scarcity value. A picture is presented of savings pouring into the industrial system through the various channels of investment, and filling up by their free circulation every avenue for the employment of capital so that all interest is forced down to a common level, the minimum rate sufficient to induce the saving public to continue the saving process. There are, however, in this description two assumptions which, so far as many employments of capital are concerned, are false. The first assumption is, that all capital can flow freely into all employments, seeking the most remunerative investment. The second is, that in no branches of industry can capital be found scarce, in comparison with land and labour. The first assumption is known to be false by every business man. Large profitable fields of industry are in every country fenced off against intruders from outside, so that the favoured capital employed therein can earn high dividends. If more capital is required by such businesses for the extension of their trade, existing shareholders or other favoured persons alone obtain the opportunity to invest it : if capital is wanted from the outside public, it is borrowed at the market rate, those who furnish it not sharing the large earnings of the company. Well-placed capitalists do not let in outsiders " on the ground floor," *i. e.* giving them any share of the high remuneration which their capital may help to " earn."

In every developed branch of modern industry some businesses enjoy a position of high remuneration for their capital: sometimes by amalgamation or by trade arrangements whole industries may be in this position. The ordinary investor either cannot put his savings into such industries, or he must buy existing shares upon terms which only secure for him a minimum return, though the seller takes in an inflated price a large anticipated future gain. In the great manufactures, in profitable mining areas, in certain branches of transport business by sea or land, in semi-public services, in some of the distributive trades, in banking, insurance and finance, there are large blocks of well-placed capital obtaining for their original or present owners rates of interest far in excess of the free competition rate. Later inquiry will indicate the nature of the advantages which such capitals enjoy. Here it is sufficient to recall the notorious fact of their existence. There does not exist that perfect freedom of competition between all owners of capital which brings all interest down to a common minimum level. Large masses of capital are lifted to various higher levels of interest. Nor can it be said that these higher earnings are passing strokes of luck or trade booms. Though all dividends are liable to fluctuate, these strong, protected businesses are less liable to fluctuate than others, and their normal average earnings over long periods of years attest their power to take " surplus."

The plain facts of modern business show that

capital like land can get a share of unproductive surplus. It gets it in the same way, through scarcity. But while land takes its surplus by a natural scarcity, capital takes its surplus by making itself scarce, *i. e.* by artificially restricting the flow of free capital into certain channels of employment. These restrictions, whether maintained by securing advantages of raw materials, power or situation, by tariffs or other State aid, by trade agreements or combinations, all signify checks upon the free entry of capital into a trade which is thus enabled to secure a scarcity rate of interest for the limited supply. Does any one suppose, for instance, that, if any company were really able to set up in England the business of banking so as to compete on equal terms with the existing banks, the earnings upon paid-up capital in that branch of industry would be what they are ? Capital put into a place of vantage, so as to be screened from free competition, sucks up surplus just the same as land. The fact that the whole of rent is " unproductive surplus," whereas part of interest is earned, must not prevent us from recognizing the identity of the two sorts of surplus. Both are unearned incomes, got because the natural scarcity of land or the contrived scarcity of capital enables the owners of the scarce factor to take all the surplus product that remains when the bare

" costs " of the more abundant factors have
been defrayed.

If the term rent be applied to all forms of
scarcity-payments to factors of production,
this surplus-interest is a rent. But· so is the
remuneration which some sorts of ability or
labour are able to secure in excess of their wage
of efficiency. Instances of groups of wage-
earners occupying a position of scarcity in
comparison with other factors of production,
and thereby enabled to take a rate of wages in
excess of the current demands of efficiency,
are not unknown. Cases occur in new countries
where plenty of good virgin soil is available
and where capital is readier to flow in than
labour. Trade-unions in well-organized trades
have sometimes been able to secure for a time
scarcity-wages in towns or districts where
capital is plentiful. But these cases will be
recognized as exceptional when a fuller
analysis of the condition of the labour market
has been presented. It is only the higher
forms of human productive energy, to which
the term " ability " is given, that show a
normal capacity to secure scarcity pay. To the
rents of land and capital may be added this
" rent of ability." Now many of those who
admit the rent of land to be unearned, and
recognize that capital may often take excessive
dividends, are apt to boggle at the view that
any part of the remuneration of ability can be

rightly included under the same head. This is due partly to the fact that whereas the landowner and the owner of capital can live idly on the proceeds of their land and capital, the man of ability often gives out continuous personal productive energy. It is generally felt not merely that he must be paid but that it is bad policy to stint his pay. Personal ability , of inventors, organizers, overseers, officials, professional men, artists, skilled technicians of every sort, must be paid upon a scale sufficient to evoke their best work, for the higher the quality of the utility of the work the greater the loss from failing to get it at its best. Since the nature of such work, its essentially intellectual, moral or artistic nature, prevents the application of the ordinary piece and time measurements which regulate the pay of most manual labour, it is felt that a generous remuneration is advisable, so as to be on the right side. Where, as has sometimes happened in the co-operative movement or in municipal services, attempts have been made to buy ability cheap, this economic lesson has been driven home by disastrous consequences.

But the difficulty and delicacy of ascertaining the rates of pay needed to sustain and evoke the various sorts of industrial ability must not lead to the conclusion that ability is necessarily worth whatever price it can get,

in the sense that it would not work as well
if it could only get a lower price. At present
in England the fee among the recognized first
rank of surgeons for a delicate and difficult
operation may be £100. A private patient
may not be able to get it done for less, and if
he has the money it may be well worth his
while to pay it. In one sense, then, it appears
to be a payment necessary to evoke the application of this sort of skill. But it may very
well be the case that in Germany this operation
is performed with equal skill for a fee of £40,
or in Switzerland for £20. Why so much
cheaper in these other countries? For two
reasons. First, because the wider spread of
opportunities of good higher and professional
education bring to the front in Germany and
Switzerland a larger proportion of natural
talent. In this way the supply of first-rate
surgical ability would be increased. On the
other hand, the proportion of rich families
able to pay a fee of £100 would be smaller in
Germany and Switzerland, so that the effective
demand for the operation at such a price would
be smaller than in England. So, with a greater
supply of this sort of ability and a smaller
demand for it at a high price, the fee must fall.
While, therefore, I must pay £100 in England
at the present time for this operation, if
improved and enlarged education brought
more first-rate surgeons to the front, I should

be able to buy the same ability for, say, £20. Although, therefore, it may appear at first sight as if the £100 fee were a wholly necessary and reasonable payment for some rare kind of natural skill, it is evident that £80 of it is simply a rent of scarcity, shifting up and down with the degree of scarcity.

Or take the case of the Town Clerk and other high officials of a large British Municipality. It is reckoned bad public policy to pay such men less than from £1000 to £1500 for their ability. But in Germany or France there is every reason to believe that men of at least as good qualifications for such posts are procured at about half the salary. The explanation is obvious, more equality of educational opportunities on the one hand, fewer opportunities to able men of entering other careers in which large surplus-incomes are frequently procurable, upon the other, bring to these official posts a larger number of well-qualified applicants. It is sometimes argued that a few high-paid places may be necessary as prizes to tempt a sufficient flow of ability into professional or business careers in which there are so many blanks. But whether applied to professional fees or to business profits, this gambling appeal is a bad economy. The low and even " sweating " salaries paid to struggling doctors and engineers can afford no economic defence of the necessity of the extremely large incomes got by a few men at the top of these professions. They are not warranted in claiming that whatever rates they are able, under the present circumstances, to obtain, are a just or permanent measure of their personal services. Indeed, it is quite evident that just as certain groups of favoured and protected capitalists can take excessive interest, so certain cliques or grades of professional, official and business men of ability can take excessive salaries, fees or profits. These payments are of the same nature as the rent of land; all are scarcity payments for a factor of production which by nature or contrivance is short in supply.

Thus interpreted, such of the surplus-product as is not distributed in costs of growth is apportioned among the owners of the several factors of production in proportion to their " pull." The particular channel into which the unproductive surplus flows varies in the various parts of the industrial system. In some countries and in some industries land is strongest and scarcest, and the bulk of the surplus goes for rent. In other countries and industries capital or ability is short and land relatively abundant; there interest or salaries and profits take more surplus.

This general conclusion as to the distribution of the surplus is conformable with common knowledge in all countries where national wealth is on the increase. The notion, for instance, that in such a country as Great Britain landlords are the residuary legatees who take in rent all surplus wealth is opposed to the plainest evidence of facts. Even the widest interpretation of " economic rent " cannot assign to it more than some fifteen per cent. of the aggregate national income, while ten per cent. is a more reasonable computation. That many wealthy families are sustained in luxury and idleness out of other sources of income than rent of land is obvious. Indeed, there is good reason to believe that the aggregate income in this country which would count as dividends or profits has during the past century grown at a far faster rate than rent. Though much of these dividends and profits may rightly count as " costs " for the upkeep and serviceable increase of the growing capital and organizing power in modern industry, there can be no question but that a great proportion is unearned or " scarcity " payment, involving no corresponding effort or sacrifice on the part of its recipients. The richest men in most advanced industrial countries to-day do not derive their riches in the main from land, but from the possession of other instruments of manufacture, transport and finance, and the control of markets.

APPENDIX

THE SOCIAL WASTE OF UNPRODUCTIVE SURPLUS

THE prominent position given in this analysis to the Unproductive Surplus makes it necessary here to clear away one misconception which is likely to arise as to the part it plays in industry. Although the rents, excessive interest and other elements which comprise this surplus, perform no useful service in stimulating the industrial activities of their recipients, it may appear that their general effect upon industry is salutary. The luxurious expenditure which they render possible imparts activity to a large number of trades, while that which is not expended but saved goes to swell the industrial capital of the nation. Therefore, though this surplus is not " productive " in the sense of sustaining or evoking the productive energy of those who receive it as " unearned income," it may be thought to be productive in its further uses, whether it be spent or saved. But a closer scrutiny disposes of this notion. For, as regards the portion that is expended upon luxuries, it adds nothing to the total volume of industry and employment. If, instead of passing as unproductive surplus to a receiver of rent or excessive profits, it were assigned by a more equitable distribution as " efficiency " wages to labour, it would still have been spent in demanding commodities. These commodities, instead of being luxuries for the rich, would have been conveniences of life for working families. Instead of increased employment being afforded in the luxury trades, the same amount of increased employment would be imparted to the trades producing working-class conveniences. But the consumption of the luxuries would contribute nothing to the working power of the industrial system, whereas the working-class expenditure would leave as a result an improved efficiency of labour-power. So much for the portion of the " unproductive surplus " spent on luxuries.

It may seem that the portion which is saved, at any rate, must be industrially beneficial. "Unproductive surplus " saved and put into new forms of capital, it may be argued, is quite as beneficial as higher wages expended in raising the efficiency of working-class families. More capital is as serviceable as more labour-power.

But it cannot be taken for granted that surplus which is saved and put into more capital is of necessity as socially serviceable as if the income which formed that surplus

had gone to raise wages and the efficiency
of labour. For we have recognized that
industrial progress depends upon a rightly
proportioned increase of the different factors
of production. If then there were a tendency
to increase new capital at a faster rate than
the efficiency of labour were increased, such
a tendency would be wasteful, regarded from
the standpoint of society. Now the " saving "
of large masses of unproductive surplus
causes just this sort of waste. For to make
large additions to the capital structure of
industry, while the efficiency of labour is
not proportionately increased, has two injurious effects. First, it upsets the adjustment of the factors of production, labour
lagging behind capital as a productive power.
Secondly, it stimulates production beyond
the pace required to supply the final commodities to consumers, and so brings about
the periodic congestions of the markets
which are seen in trade depressions. This is
the inevitable result of a distribution which
creates unproductive surplus out of income
needed to raise the efficiency of wage-earners.
For the rising consumption of the wage-
earners, who form the vast majority of
consumers, is necessary in order to take out
of the industrial system the increasing quantity of consumables which its growing powers
enable it to produce. That is to say, out

of the surplus product in a progressive society only a limited quantity of income can advantageously be put into new capital, the rest being needed to raise the general volume of consumption so as to furnish full employment for this new capital and the new labour-power which such a distribution will evoke. The chief waste attending the accumulation of unproductive surplus is that it causes an excess of the new capital to come into being, plant of various sorts being increased so fast that an attempt to work the industrial system thus overloaded soon brings about a glut, followed by a fall of prices and a stoppage of industrial processes, which continues until the glut has been worked off, and trade reviving, the same vicious round of under-consumption, over-saving, over-production and consequent depression again recurs.

CHAPTER VII

WAGES

LABOUR stands on so different a footing from the other factors of production in regard to the conditions of its sale that a separate law of wages has often been propounded. Such procedure, however, is quite un-warranted. For the price of labour is determined like the price of the other factors by considerations of cost and scarcity affecting the relation of the supply to the demand. (Supply means the quantity of anything offered for sale within a given time at the current price, or the rate at which anything is put upon the market. Demand means the quantity of anything bought within a given time at the current price, or the rate at which anything is withdrawn by buyers.) But while there is no special law of wages, there are conditions peculiar to the sale of labour, which deserve a separate discussion. Unlike land and capital, labour cannot be detached from the person of its owner. When its productive power is used, this use requires the presence of the owner on the spot, and commonly entails certain effects upon his liberty and life which are not easily or adequately counted in the cost. Risk to life or limb, incident upon employment, seldom figures in the wages bargain, while dirt, disease or degrading character of work have little influence upon the rate of pay. The wage-earner can seldom, like the landlord or the capitalist, withhold the offer of his productive agent for a while so as to raise its price. For, in the first place, he has usually no other means of livelihood to keep him while he waits. Secondly, if he could wait, his waiting would not merely waste his labour in the interval, but, by the starvation and the idleness it entailed, would damage the efficiency of his labour afterwards. The employer, the capitalist, the landlord, can wait, for they have a reserve on which to live, and, though their waiting involves some present loss, they can usually recover it in the terms which they are able to exact when they once more apply their land or capital which has not suffered any wastage of productive efficiency from a temporary withdrawal.

Most workers, in a word, must sell their labour continuously for whatever it will fetch. But the natural condition of the labour-market has another disadvantage for the sellers. Their labour is contained in a large number of little separate pieces : the capital is usually concentrated in large masses wielded by a few employers. The sellers of labour, then, are many, the buyers few. This is an obvious advantage to the buyers, whose competition with one another is likely to be less free and continuous. Though it is the object of trade-unionism by collective bargaining to turn the edge of this natural disadvantage, it can only succeed by maintaining a more complete solidarity of labour than that which the employers can achieve by their combination. Now employers, being fewer and better informed, can usually maintain a stronger organization than labour, with a far larger reserve in case of hostilities. Again, where labour is more successful, the conditions of its powerful combination usually involve so rigorous a guard on the trade entrances as to increase the difficulty of an equally effective combination for other sorts of labour. This brings us to the central defect in the capacity of labour as a claimant for the " surplus product." For the distribution of this surplus, as we saw, depends upon the scarcity of the respective factors. Now land is attended by a natural scarcity, only to be overcome partially and with difficulty. Capital acquires a position of scarcity by organized contrivance. Ability has some natural and some contrived capacity. But labour is naturally abundant and has shown no adequate power to establish and maintain scarcity of supply.

A few rare local instances have occurred, in the building or carrying trade of some American city, or among the shearers or other season workers of some new low-populated country, where a combination of labour has for a brief time enjoyed the same advantages of shortage which the ground-landlords of every large city, the employers in every well-organized industry, enjoy all the time. But the normal continuous condition of labour in most countries is one of over-supply, in the sense that there is usually more labour offered than is bought. Labour is the only factor of which the supply generally and permanently exceeds the demand. Though restraints upon the birth-rate and improved organization of workers doubtless tend to diminish this over-supply, they have not got rid of it. And so long as any over-supply exists, its necessary effect, so far as free competition operates, is to drag down wages to that lower level which covers bare costs of maintenance, or such slightly higher level as law, public opinion, custom or humanity prescribes. For if there are thirteen men competing for twelve jobs, the

struggle of each to escape being the excluded
one will drive the price of labour to a minimum nearly as effectually as if there were
twenty men competing instead of thirteen.
We may, then, summarize the general conditions which distinguish the labour-market
from the markets for the sale of other factors,
by saying that labour is naturally more
abundant than the other factors and is less
capable of correcting its abundance by
organized contrivance.

A clear understanding of the nature of the
wage bargain compels us to look more closely
to the relation of the individual worker to
the labour-problem. In our general statement of the price of labour as a " cost " we
assumed that the price could not be less than
would suffice to keep the worker in his ordinary health and strength, and enable him to
support a family sufficient to replace him
when his working time was over. In a
progressive industrial society wages must be
higher than this mere " wear and tear "
pay, including a stimulus and maintenance
of more labour-power for the growth of
industry. If every family were of about
the same size and were supported entirely
by a single wage-earner, an intelligible theory
of wages might be constructed on this basis.
But neither of these conditions is fulfilled.
Working-class families vary in size and in

the number of their members who are earning
wages. Now, from the standpoint both of
the industrial system and of humanity, the
subsistence or efficiency wage means the
weekly income of the family. There is, however, nothing in the conditions of the single
wage bargain to ensure this family subsistence. For what is sold in that bargain is a
given quantity of productive power. The
same price is given for a unit of this power,
whether it is given out by a man who must
support a wife and six children out of the
price he gets, by a man who has only himself
to keep, or by a man whose wife and children
are all earning money. If the wage were
a full maintenance for the first case, it would
yield a surplus for the second, and a still
larger surplus for the third family. If, on
the other hand, it is only sufficient for the
single worker, then the man supporting a
family out of it is evidently " sweated " and
unable to maintain his own and his family's
efficiency.

It is true that by process of bargaining there
is some tendency to fix a wage sufficient to
defray the ordinary, or average, expenses the
worker has to meet. In most male employments, for instance, wages must lie somewhere
above the amount needed to support a single
man, for otherwise married men with families
to keep would not work in those trades and

the supply of labour would be deficient. So, in most metal or mining centres, wages for men are somewhat higher for the same level of skill than in textile towns where there is fuller and more remunerative employment for women and children. But though thus indirectly there is some tendency to make wages conform to the needs of family subsistence, the tendency is exceedingly defective. Whereas a vigorous young Lancashire operative may, while unmarried, earn a weekly wage that yields a surplus on his needs, when married with a young family to keep he often finds the same wage deficient for their proper maintenance, while afterwards, if he still keeps his earning power when they are old enough to get employment, he may once more find his wages adequate to meet his needs. This fact that maintenance of labour depends on the composite family wage, while the wage bargain regards merely the quantity of labour power given out by the individual worker, is the greatest crux of the wages question. The typical wage bargain for the price of labour per piece or per hour, is doubly defective from the sound economic standpoint. It does not secure a weekly wage for the continuous subsistence of the individual worker, much less does it secure the whole or any fixed proportion of the family subsistence. Yet, from the standpoint of the industrial system, it is this last fact that is essential.

Even where family needs have some indirect influence in fixing individual wages, ordinary family conditions alone count. The wage-system cannot take into account the shoals of exceptional cases, where the family is larger than usual, where there is an invalid wife or sickly children, or where the death or disability of the chief wage-earner throws the entire support of the family upon the woman.

This last consideration brings up the special features of the labour bargain in the case of women. Its most onerous effects fall more heavily on women than on men. For the fact that the male wage is based in part upon a loose principle that a man is the sole or chief support of a family, while a woman is not, exercises a depressing influence on the price of female labour. In most work the earnings of a man would anyhow be greater, because of the larger amount of productive power he can give out. But this assumption, that the man supports others while the woman does not, has operated to raise male wages to a higher level over female wages for similar work than would otherwise have happened. It has helped to make the customary wage of men about twice that of women, instead of, perhaps, one-third more.

The assumption, otherwise expressed, is that every woman is partially supported by some man. The depressing effect of this assumption is such that the ordinary wage for able-bodied efficient women-workers in most skilled and unskilled trades is below the level of separate maintenance. It is not a question of some low-skilled, irregular, home industry like matchbox-making or shirt-making. The ordinary woman's wage regarded as the sole source of her income is a sweating wage. The 10s. or 12s., the usual factory wage outside Lancashire, is not enough to keep a woman living by herself in full efficiency and to enable her to provide against ordinary emergencies. Far more cruel is the effect of the wage-system on the large number of women who have to keep not merely themselves but a family out of their earnings, for they feel the full brunt of a system of bargaining which may drive the piece-wage or the weekly-wage of the individual worker indefinitely below subsistence point. Though this is no place for discussing remedies for industrial diseases, it may be pointed out that the mere insistence, either by legal or co-operative action, that women shall be paid at the same rate for the same work as men, would not, by itself, be likely to do very much to raise the industrial status or the wages of women.

For, in the first place, there are not many occupations in which women are doing identical work with men. Again, where they are doing the same or nearly the same work, they usually hold that employment on the condition of taking lower wages, and if, by legal or trade-union pressure, they insisted upon equal pay with men, they would be driven from the trade. Finally, if we are regarding wages from the social-economic standpoint as maintenance, since most women have not to contribute so much as men to the family maintenance, it is not so obviously just and desirable, as it sometimes seems, that they should be paid as highly as men even for the same work. Looking at labour as a mere commodity it seems equitable that the same price for it should be paid to female sellers as to male. But looking at it as a means of support for a working family, it is more important that the chief wage-earner should be highly paid than that the same rate should be paid to the subsidiary wage-earner. Only in as far as the growing economic activity of women tends to make her as important a factor in the earning of the family income as the man, is it obviously desirable that the same rate of pay should prevail. This conditional defence of the higher rate for men, however, does not dispose of the numerous cases where the woman,

not the man, bears the whole or the chief
burden of supporting the family. These
numerous exceptions require exceptional treatment which, if the competitive wage-system
is not competent to accord, should be a matter
for public provision. The fact that women
are physically debarred from many highly-
paid employments, and that the chronic
over-supply of the labour in those open to
them forces them to underbid men and one
another for wage-work, cannot be adequately
met by a policy of equal pay for equal work,
and unless a public provision for unemployed
women formed a foundation for co-operative
action among wage-earners, the enforcement
of this general maxim of equality might
seriously worsen women's economic condition.
This will suffice to show that, whereas the
conditions for the sale of the use of land and
capital must always be such as to make
provision for full maintenance of these factors,
the conditions of the labour bargain do not
necessarily secure the subsistence of the
single worker or the working-class family.
If individual bargaining were general, and
the economic forces above described had
unrestricted sway, the condition of the wage-
earners as a body would be much worse than
it actually is. There are, however, counter-
forces to be taken into account. The most
important of these is the intelligent self-

interest of the employer. In many trades it would not really pay the employer to buy all his labour at the cheapest rate at which he could get men to work. For certain qualities of personal efficiency, affecting the quality of skill, intelligence, responsibility, etc., could not be got from " sweated " labour. The good-will of the workers also enables a business to be run more smoothly and with less supervision. The recognition of these obvious facts has caused a policy, which was always applied to salaried officials in public or in private business, to be extended in many cases to the better grades of wage-earners. This policy is sometimes called " the economy of high wages," and is based on the truth that if you pay a man a higher rate, you will get more or better work out of him. For he will be able to give out more labour-power by reason of the higher standard of physical and intellectual comfort his wages allow him to support, and he will be willing to do so, because he will recognize himself as having a personal stake in the success of the business. Sometimes this extra-wage is given by some " bonus " or " profit-sharing " method. But it always tends to raise the family-wage above the point of bare subsistence and to stimulate increased efficiency of labour.

Some have laid so much stress on this policy

as to suggest that if employers could all be got
to recognize its full validity, high wages and
short hours would generally prevail, and all
conflicts between capital and labour would
disappear. But this is a view that ignores
important qualifications of the policy. For
there are many cases where " sweating " is
a more profitable present policy for the
employer than high wages. In most of the
domestic workshops and other low-organized
businesses where women or " green " male
hands are employed, it would not be profitable to pay anything but sweating wages.
Even under the factory system and in many
offices and retail stores, there are large
numbers of workers on starvation or bare
subsistence wages who would not respond
to higher wages in a proportionate amount
of increased productivity. It is foolish to
pretend that sweating is always an unenlightened policy from the profit-making standpoint. So long as there stands a plentiful
supply of idle hands, ready to take the place
of the labour exhausted or used up, it is
often " good business " to pay the lowest
market price for low-skilled labour. Again,
where there is some disposition among better
employers to pay a higher wage which would
come home later on in increased efficiency,
the competition of greedier or shorter-sighted
rivals often prevents its application.

E

While, then, it is indisputable that this factor has played an important part in raising the standard of wages and of comfort in the skilled artisan classes, it cannot be relied upon to secure for labour in general an adequate wage of progressive efficiency. Perhaps its chief effect has been to co-operate with the forces of public opinion, trade-union action and industrial legislation, so as to help to build up and maintain a number of different levels of working-class comfort, roughly corresponding to the skill and intelligence involved in the various staple trades.

It is important to recognize the causes and supports of these higher grades of wages and of the standards of living which depend on them. Some sorts of labour are more arduous, more disagreeable, more degrading, more dangerous than others, and it might seem natural that these disadvantages must be offset by a higher rate of pay. But this is seldom the case. For unless these disadvantages are of such character as positively to exclude the ordinary worker from competing for the employment, they do not apparently raise the wage-level. Most heavy, dirty, repulsive, unhealthy labour is paid for at the lowest rates, because the over-supply of low-skilled workers of average capacity is such that they cannot afford to take these conditions into consideration. Only when some unusually high standard of physique is necessary, as in the case of certain stevedores and foundry workers, does the arduous nature of the work tell upon the rate of wages. Danger or degradation hardly counts until it reaches the limit of the steeplejack or the hangman. This statement, however, requires one qualification. Though heavy, disagreeable, or dirty work seldom gets paid at a much higher rate, light, easy and genteel conditions, on the other hand, especially for women, depress wages below the ordinary. This partly explains the low pay of ordinary clerks and shop-assistants. The only large employment in which personal feelings much affect wages is domestic service, where servility and loss of independence are compensated by relatively high pay. Trades involving skill, intelligence and responsibility, generally have higher levels of wages. To some extent this is doubtless due to the consideration already adduced, viz. that a certain level of comfort and security conduces to the efficiency of these sorts of labour. But a more important cause is the relative scarcity of numbers of workers qualified to do such work. When the working classes had little access to ordinary schooling, the wages of clerical skill were relatively high; free popular education has pulled them down, not because

less skill and knowledge are needed for a
modern clerk, but because a larger proportion
of young men and women are able to attain
these qualifications. In a word, skill, intelligence and other personal qualities, like
the positive disagreeabilities attaching to
various kinds of work, can only raise the
wage-level in one of two ways, either by
requiring a higher standard of subsistence
for the physical or mental energy to be given
out, or by restricting the number of qualified
applicants in the labour-market.

A main purpose of trade-unionism has been
to assist these two tendencies. By helping
to maintain higher levels of class comfort for
the grades of skilled workers, and by resisting
the downward pressure exercised by bad or
unenlightened employers, or by organizations
of employers in bad times of trade, they have
assisted to maintain the labour conditions
essential for industrial progress. The particular restrictions upon entrance into a trade,
upon output and the use of machinery,
have all been directed to maintain a relative
scarcity of labour in the trade, without
which collective bargaining would be in-
effective. Parts of this policy have been
shortsighted and mistaken, as regards the
immediate interests of the workers concerned,
especially the resistance to labour-saving
machines in trades, where, as in printing,

cheapening of production would quickly
stimulate demand so largely as to enhance
the aggregate employment in the trade.
But even here the circumstances of each
trade must be taken into account. While
labour-saving machines and other economies
tend, in the long run and as regards the
general body of the workers, to raise wages
without diminishing employment, the method
of their introduction under the spur of competitive profit-seeking is often truly detrimental to special bodies of workers immediately affected; and though the " long run "
may bring compensations, the narrow margin
of their lives and means compel them to
safeguard as far as possible the " short run."
Nor is the resistance of organized wage-
earners to rapid changes of method justifiable
merely from the standpoint of their immediate group-interests. It is justifiable also
from the wider social-economic standpoint,
provided the resistance is gradually relaxed.
For the swift wholesale changes which competitive profit-seeking often prompts, are
fraught with wider social and industrial
dangers. So far as trade-union opposition
only moderates the pace of these industrial
changes, it not merely serves its own interests,
but incidentally the social interest.

Industrial laws, regulating the hours of
labour and other conditions in different

trades to various extents, assist in making the scarcity and the organization of labour more effective in some trades than in others, and so in raising and maintaining the different levels of standard wages which we find. If there had been no factory laws, no Acts protecting the lives of workers, or discriminating age or sex for purposes of employment, the incentives which evoked those improvements of machinery and methods that demand higher qualities of skill and morale in factory workers, would have been far weaker than they have been, and the opportunities, of which the higher grades of specialized labour have availed themselves for organization, would not have existed.

Thus we see how a combination of technical conditions, legislation and organization, has removed labour from a common low level, disposing it in a series of graded terraces, with rising standards of wages and of comfort. No modern treatment of the wages question can take labour as a single market amenable to some one " iron law " or other simple formula.

There are many sorts of labour, each with its own market and its own price, just as we saw there were many markets for the use of land and capital. Though the young raw labourer has some choice of occupation, for most workers this choice is very restricted both as regards trade and locality. The lower grades, requiring low skill and training, are more accessible to one another, so that we may speak of " labourers " in towns as if they formed a single market and had a single price, which indeed is substantially the case. The same is true of women's factory work in all but the most highly skilled trades. The degree of skill wanted can be acquired so readily by most young women that in effect a single market and a single price exists. The higher the skill or quality of the labour, the smaller the proportion of the ripening wage-earners able to qualify and enter this labour-market, and the more inaccessible it is to workers hitherto engaged in other sorts of work. So, for skilled male labour there exists a number of very distinct labour-markets, protected against rushes from outside, and so less likely to be hampered by a large permanent excess of supply. Wage-earners in this condition, being more intelligent and better paid, are enabled to organize themselves for bargaining far more effectively than wage-earners in the lower grades. So they are able to raise the level of their wages to a larger extent than the mere superiority of skill would appear to warrant. Because a compositor may on the average earn a wage twice as high as a cotton or woollen weaver, one is not entitled to assume that the work he does is twice as skilful. What mainly determines the wage-level is the plenty or scarcity of the supply of available labour in the trade, not the degree of skill required, except so far as the latter condition affects the former. As in the use of land and capital, scarcity of supply is the direct determinant of the price of the various sorts of labour. As in the case of capital, so in that of labour, it is the chief object of organization to procure and maintain scarcity by making it difficult for outside labour easily to enter the trade, and by restraining full freedom of competition inside the trade.

The establishment of a number of wage-levels for different trades does not, of course, signify that all the workers in the same trade tend to earn the same amount of money in a week or in a year. As more productive land or capital gets higher rent or interest than less productive in the same employment, so it is usually the case with labour. Where piece-wages prevail, this is, of course, obvious. A quicker or a better worker will take in a day or a week a larger sum, representing the larger size of his output or the smaller deduction for faulty work. Since a quicker or better worker gets more out of a machine, he will also often get in addition to the wage a bonus which merely measures the greater quantity of piece-work done. These differences of individual earnings will vary very greatly in accordance with the conditions of the work. Where the machine closely sets the pace, and only those are employed who are competent to follow machines well speeded up, the individual differences of earnings will not be large. But where pace is largely or entirely a matter of individual deftness or nervous energy, one worker at the same piece-rate will often earn twice the money that another earns.

These individual differences of earnings correspond to the difference of rent which follow the differences of fertility in acres of land, or the differences of interest which follow different hundred pounds of capital well or ill invested.

In every industry at any given time there is some labour, as there is some land and capital, which is only just worth while employing at the market price. This labour, land or capital, is said to be " on the margin " of employment. When wheat prices in England fell below 30s. per quarter some years ago, large tracts of poorer wheat land in Essex and elsewhere went out of cultivation, to be brought under the plough again when wheat prices rose, as it became once more worth while buying these acres back from pasture. So in many manufactories there are machines which, being somewhat out of date, are not

E 2

worked in ordinary times. But when a pressure of orders comes and good prices prevail, it pays to bring these once more into operation. Most labour markets contain, though they do not maintain, a similar reserve of labour, somewhat inferior to the average labour employed in ordinary times, but brought into temporary use in periods of booming trade.

For every industry that is not a close monopoly more land, labour and capital is usually available than is in actual use. That is to say, there exist portions of the factors which lie below the present margin of employment. This does not necessarily mean that they are not employed at all. They may be employed in some other industry. Acres of land not good enough for growing wheat at present wheat prices may be used for grazing cattle; workers not good enough for getting coal may be employed in agricultural labour. But if the price of wheat makes it worth while, some of this pasture land will be brought into arable use; if the price of coal impels the opening of more pits, some rural labour will be drafted into coal-mining.

For the higher price of wheat or coal will make it worth while to use land or labour less productive than the worst formerly in use, and to pay a price high enough to bring in the necessary quantity from some other employment if there is not enough lying unemployed.

So we must recognize that for every industry employing land, capital and labour of different grades or qualities, there exists a supply of all these factors, either lying idle or put to some other use, which is not good enough at the present price that must be paid to get them, but which will be brought into the industry if a rise of prices of the product of the industry makes it profitable to employ them. The marginal land, labour or capital in any trade will thus shift with the more or less remunerative condition of the trade.

This moving up and down of " margins " in the factors of production is the actual process by which each trade feeds itself with the increased quantity of labour, or capital, or land it needs for its growth. Of course some of the new land or capital thus brought in may, after it has been acquired, prove to be as productive as that in former use. The fact that formerly it was below the margin, in the sense of not being worth using at the price, often means that some preliminary barrier has been overcome. For some land below the margin is more fertile than some land in use, but it costs a good deal to clear and prepare it. Some agricultural labour may make excellent mining labour but will take time and training. So it appears that trades and businesses compete with one another not only for the increased factors of production but for those in use. This competition, in fact, is the usual way in which the industrial system tries to put the proper quantity of land, capital, labour and ability in the places where each can be most profitably employed. So far as profitable employment corresponds with productive employment, and only to that extent, this competitive ordering of the factors secures the maximum production of wealth. This leads to a consideration of the part played by the business man, the person directly responsible for ordering the factors of production for the attainment of profit.

CHAPTER VIII

PROFITS

THE business man directly engaged in organizing the processes of industry is sometimes described as the capitalist-employer, because he owns or controls the capital and hires the labour in a business. But it is not as owner of capital that he here concerns us. For, though the controller of a modern business may own the whole or part of the capital, such possession is not essential to him as business man. Indeed in the big organized joint-stock businesses the detailed control or management is often in the hands of men who own little or none of the capital.

The typical business man hires his capital as he hires his labour, paying the current rate of interest for it. His practice is to buy the use of the labour, capital and land he wants at the lowest market prices, organize their co-operation in some productive process, and sell the products at a price which leaves a margin after defraying his expenses of production. This margin represents his pay-

ment for his business ability. It is usually
termed his "profit," and we shall reserve
this word to describe the payment for the
ability or energy which he and other business
men apply. But one may as well admit that
popular usage has given such loose and shifty
meanings to the word as to make its use in
a scientific work very difficult. It is liable,
in the first place, to be confused with interest,
for where a business man owns his own capital
he is apt to include the interest on that
capital in his net profit. Indeed, in the
book-keeping of a private business there is
usually no attempt to distinguish the two.
Or profit may also include a payment for the
risks to which the capital is exposed, though
that should properly be accounted for as
insurance cost. Moreover, managerial salaries,
directors' fees and bonuses, form part of the
true net profit though not usually included
in it. Finally, a good deal of profit goes to
enhance dividends in enterprises where the
terms on which the capital was raised are
such as enable the shareholders to benefit
by the skilled management or good fortune
of the undertaking.

But after due allowance is made for these
irregularities of use, it will be convenient to
regard the business men who organize and
control the industrial processes as taking
in the form of net profits the margin that

remains after all expenses are defrayed. A
great variety of energy and ability goes into
the work of this business man. He is responsible for planning the size and structure of
the business, deciding' what plant is to be
used, what processes employed, and how
much labour of different sorts. He next
must hire the requisite capital and labour,
organize its co-operation for the processes
of production, and buy the proper sorts of
materials on favourable terms : the final
product he must market advantageously.
These processes of buying and selling, of
technical business organization, the control
of labour, and the book-keeping and finance,
require a combination of sagacity, knowledge, enterprise, industry and self-command,
the virtues of the good business man. Where
large quantities of other people's money are
involved, honesty and a high sense of responsibility are important ingredients of the
business character. Much of this work only
demands, however, a sort of ability which
is tolerably plentiful in any civilized country
where ordinary means of education are
widely available. So a manager of a mill
in a staple trade can usually be selected from
an ample supply of qualified applicants at a
salary not greatly exceeding the wages of
foremen or skilled artisans in the best-paid
processes of manual labour.

Although this ordinary work of management involves many acts of judgment which contribute to the success or failure of the business, it may be regarded as tolerably routine in character, and as distinct from the critical plans and judgments formed by the man responsible for the general direction of the business.

This business man is thus a link between the producer (or owner of a productive agent) and the consumer. His work consists in arranging and conducting the most economical co-operation of various sorts of capital and labour, and his pay, or profit, consists of the difference between the expenses of buying the factors of production and the price he can get for the product. At first sight it may appear as if he were merely a mercantile middleman, buying something cheap and selling it dear. But even among commercial business men there are few whose profitable operations merely amount to this. For the merchant organizes distribution, gathering his various goods from different sources, selecting and arranging them, and placing them at the disposal of retailers in greater quantities and ampler choice than would be possible if each retailer had himself to seek producers of each article he needed to stock his shop. The middleman who thrusts himself needlessly and officiously between two classes of producer, or between producer and consumer, is the exception, not the rule, though it is true that many middlemen consume their energy more in competition with one another than in the proper part which belongs to them, the organization of markets.

But the head of a manufacturing firm, the manager of a railway or of a mine, performs a more obviously productive operation. The separate bits of capital and labour that he buys only attain their full productive power when they are brought together. The whole is more productive than the mere sum of the productive value of the parts. A worker, say a carpenter or shoemaker, can produce very little by himself, or with such tools, material and market as he can himself command : only when he is brought into a fully equipped business, with all the advantages of division of labour and specialized capital, are his energy and skill fully productive.

If, then, a business man can buy his labour at a price which represents its small productivity as a single unit, and sell the greatly enlarged product which comes from using it with other units of labour and of capital, he will appear to make an immense gain in actual wealth which he can take for his profit.

This indeed is what he tries to do, and, as

we saw, there is a socialistic theory which
virtually explains all " surplus " as consisting in this sort of gain. But there are
several considerations which prevent the full
acceptance of this explanation of " surplus."
In the first place, the business man does the
same thing with the capital he uses in his
business. A typical modern business requires
him to collect from many different little men
of capital, investors, a number of bits of
capital. Each of these by itself is much less
productive than when he has organized it
into his business structure. Here, too, he
seems to buy it at a price measuring its
smaller separate productivity, to make it
more productive by combination, and to keep
to himself the whole gain, or profit, of the
proceeding.

Thus there seems to be a surplus value got
out of capital corresponding to that got by
buying labour cheap. And it is quite true
that profit may be taken to consist of the
difference between the smaller productivity of
labour and capital used in other ways and the
larger productivity when applied to the
organized business in question.

If a business man could really get and keep
for himself as profit all the difference between
what a worker, or £100 of capital, could
produce " by itself " and what he or it could
produce as a factor of an organized business,

profits would swallow up the whole of any industrial surplus that could be found. But no business man can get all this. For he finds other business men bent upon the same object. This competition checks profit in two ways. The first business man who came among a population of small peasants and set them working in a factory or mine would get them at a wage slightly exceeding what they could earn each working for himself upon the soil. The aggregate increase in the product of their labour would be great, and he would be able to keep nearly all of it as profit. The early " clothiers " and other factory owners did in fact get this advantage when they exploited a locality hitherto untouched by the new industry. But, as other business men came into the same field, their surplus-profit was liable to be cut into at both ends. For our clothier could no longer always buy labour at a price just above the agricultural earnings, but found himself bidding against other business men trying to do the same thing. In order to get the labour he wanted he was obliged to pay a wage slightly exceeding, not the agricultural earnings, but the wage it was worth while another factory owner to offer to the peasant. In other words, when his available supply of raw labour was limited and a good many business men were beginning to exploit it, its price would rise so as to cause a rise in the cost of working the factory or mine.

And what applies to labour would in some measure apply also to capital and land. The first-comer among the business men would evidently get the land for building a factory, or for working minerals, on easier terms than afterwards, when other business firms were competing for the best sites or the likeliest seams. So competition among business men in buying the factors of production will keep down profits by raising expenses. The same cause will cut down profits at the other end, by reducing the price at which the product of the factory or mine is marketed. The first-comer here again has the pull. For he not only buys his labour and other factors cheap, but he can sell his product dear, so long as he remains alone in the field. But as the competition of other business men becomes effective in the market for his products, as well as in the labour market, he finds his handsome profit, *i. e.* the difference between the low price of the factors and the high price of his product, cut down simultaneously at both ends. If the competition becomes not merely effective but intense, his profit may be reduced to a bare minimum.

Thus, as a matter of mere theory, the business man, as the owner of a factor of production, viz. business ability, appears to be in the same position as the owner of any of the other factors. Scarcity or monopoly may yield him a large surplus of unearned income, abundance or competition may reduce his " profit " to a minimum just sufficing to evoke the use of his business ability.

In practice profits vary so much more than wages, or interest or salaries, for the same sort of organizing work in the same trades, that it seems as if no general statement could be applied to them. In certain trades some well-equipped businesses will be taking very high rates of profit, others very low. The difference is commonly put down to the ability of direction and management. Where two manufacturing businesses, two large hotels, two retail general stores, are worked with adequate capital under the same external conditions, and one succeeds while the other fails, it seems evident that either luck or skill of management must explain the difference. Though luck plays a larger part in the business world than is sometimes supposed, management is commonly accounted the efficient cause. And this is doubtless a true view. But to jump from this view to the theory that the creative power of business ability has brought into being a great fund of wealth which belongs to the business man, as the necessary reward of his superior mental energy and skill, fails to take into account the full conditions of such business success.

Take an illustration most favourable to this superstitious view of human ability, the case of two equally well-situated hotels or shops, one of which gets high profits while the other only just pays its way. Ability of management undoubtedly has a great deal to do with the difference of result. This ability will operate in two directions. The successful business will be better organized, *i. e.* the capital and labour will be better chosen and better directed. But a little reflection enables one to see that, though the initiative in this better organization may proceed from the ability of the single manager, its efficacy depends upon the capacity of all the various employees for co-operating to carry out the manager's directions. In other words, there is a sort of ability which oozes from the whole organized personnel of the business to help towards success. This cannot be ignored, it is not merely a condition but a joint-agent in the success. Every just-minded manager of a successful business recognizes that a large share of his success is due to the co-operation of his subordinates or employees. Again, much of the success of the hotel or shop will be due to the fact that it has gathered a special clientele who think they can buy there some quality of article or some comfort or accommodation which they cannot get elsewhere. This superiority is often very slight, often indeed a mere matter of form or fashion, resting on no substantial basis of merit, but it serves to lift a business out of the ruck of competition, and secure it a control of the market.

The whole profit of a successful business, beyond what is really minimum wages of ability, is a scarcity rent or surplus, attributable, like every other surplus, to a restraint upon free competition by limiting the supply of the factor of production that receives the surplus. The conduct of modern industry lends itself to this scarcity. For, though there is most likely a plentiful natural supply of efficient business ability of various orders, only a small proportion of its owners can find an opportunity of training and applying it. Many men of natural ability cannot get it recognized, or cannot get the confidence of men with capital needed for their gift to fructify, or they cannot find or make a good business opportunity for employing it. There may be thousands of men fitted by nature to be heads of a great shipping firm or of a banking company, but the number of men required for such posts is counted by tens. The small number of effective competing firms in many of the highly-developed enterprises means that many of the profitable orders or contracts are not really made the subject of close bargaining. They pass to one or other of the firms that has acquired a special reputation for "that class of business," or else the competition of the few firms competent to undertake the work is qualified by combination or arrangement. So a very large quantity of work is done on terms yielding a rate of profit far in excess of what would have been got if such competition operated as prevails between rival grocers in the same street.

The same paucity of the number of close-competing firms, of course, not only raises selling prices but lowers the price of labour and of free capital. For it is evident that labour can get better terms, if there exists a number of keenly competing firms bidding for the best supply, than if there are only half-a-dozen whose profitable state stimulates them to organize a strong employers' association. A general survey of the industrial world would perhaps distinguish the trades where close competition is maintained between considerable numbers of standardized routine businesses from those where each business does a more or less separate class of work and has a market that is to some extent its own. Both may belong to great capitalist enterprise, but the ordinary profits of the former will be low, while many businesses of the latter class will be able to make great profits even in the ordinary course of trade.

It is probable that in advanced industrial countries, such as Great Britain and the United States, a constantly increasing share of the " surplus " figures as net profits to the successful " business man." This statement is probably correct, even if full allowance is made for losses of unsuccessful " business men." Of the aggregate " surplus " which we term " unproductive " because it exceeds the necessary inducement to apply a factor of production, business ability takes a considerably larger share than land or capital.

The justification of this statement would involve a more minute examination than is here possible, and it would be necessary to include under profits a good deal that is concealed under interest and rent. But it is supported by a general appeal to experience. Most of the families of evidently growing wealth have made their wealth out of " trade." By this is meant that profits, rather than rent or interest, constitutes the origin and substance of their wealth. Part of this wealth may reasonably be regarded as the costs of ability, the remuneration necessary to evoke and encourage the larger quantity and variety of business skill which modern industry requires. But a large part will rank with economic rent of land and surplus interest as "unproductive surplus." The general trend of modern industrial development has been to assign more importance, more power and more wealth, to the employing and directing class. "Capitalists," as such, though increasing in numbers and in the amount of capital they own, are of relatively less importance. They have become investors, and though they take in interest a large share of the whole product, their control even of the use of the capital they own is diminishing and passing more and more into the hands of directors and employers.

But an understanding of the modern system would be very imperfect if it did not include a special consideration of one particular species of "business men," viz. those concerned with the general organization of industry by means of finance. For as the ordinary little capitalist is in effect controlled by the managers of the business he has put his money in, so the latter are in an increasing measure the dependents and agents of great financial houses.

The business man, as such, is not an inventor of new processes. The ability of a Stevenson, an Edison, a Siemens, belongs to a different order. Only when it has been

acquired and taken over by a business man
does it rank as industrial power. Of course
some inventors are also business men and so
are able to exploit industrially their genius.
But these are rare exceptions. The ability
of the business man requires, not that he
should invent, but that he should have a
true eye for the business value of other
people's inventions. This, in fact, should be
considered as his first function in an age
of progress. He is the man with an eye for
profitable notions, whether the notion be a
new machine, a new product, a new market,
or a new business method. He will distinguish profitable from unprofitable notions,
buy the former as cheaply as he can, make or
adopt a business structure to embody his
notion, and get his profit by conducting such
a business or by selling it to some other
business man. Most of these notions are
industrially productive as well as profitable.
When a mechanical invention cheapens manufacture, or transport, or introduces a new
comfort or convenience of life, utilizes a
waste product, or opens up a new market,
the inventor or series of inventors and the
business man between them have been directly
instrumental in causing an addition to the
world's wealth. Other notions equally profitable to the business man may, however,
carry little or no industrial productivity.

An artful mode of advertising, a cheap parasitic imitation of an established article, a skilful method of company promotion, may be quite as profitable, though destitute of any productivity. It may be just as profitable to get business away from another firm as to establish a new business, and though upon the average this success in competition implies the substitution of a somewhat better or cheaper article, there are many cases where no such gain can be assumed.

Where business ability is thus applied to the exploitation of a profitable notion, that exploitation may be achieved in a single stroke or by a longer business process. The financial dealer in profitable notions promotes or reconstructs a company, sometimes taking out at once in cash, or in shares which he at once " unloads," as much as he can of the anticipated future profits of the working of the company. Sometimes he retains a holding of shares, using them either to earn dividends or for profitable dealing on the Stock Exchange. The part played by this type of business man is of rapidly growing importance in modern industry, and the proportion of the general wealth which passes to him as " profit " is increasing.

In countries where joint-stock enterprise is most highly developed, as in Great Britain

and America, it is probably the case that
three-quarters of the fresh supply of capital
goes into companies and pays heavy toll to
the financial organizers. This profit, however, though often excessive, is by no means
all unearned. For under our competitive
system the financier is an indispensable
being, and upon the skilled performance of
his will the economical working of the industrial system more and more depends. Though
he is " out for profit," the work for which he is
paid consists in the direction of the new supply
of industrial energy to the places where it is
wanted for the growth of the industrial system. For the money or paper values, with
which financiers seem to be exclusively concerned, are the machinery by which not only
real capital but labour and business ability
are drawn to the industrial points where they
can be productively applied. The floating
of a bogus rubber company, by which investors are duped into entrusting their savings to financial sharpers who use them for
their private purposes, is the exception not
the rule. The proper work of the financier
is to cause money-savings to take shape in
steam engines and steel rails for a Canadian
railway, dynamos for some electric-power
company, spinning-frames and factory buildings for a textile company, and to draw
from the general supply of labour a sufficient

number of the right sort of workers to co-operate with these various sorts of plant.

Now that a larger and larger number of the staple trades are passing under joint-stock enterprise, while the apparatus for gathering and conveying capital and labour is becoming more complex and more wide-spread, it follows that the work of financial direction grows more delicate and more important. Firms like J. P. Morgan's, Rothschild's, and the like, are engaged in directing the flow of immense streams of new industrial energy to various parts of the earth, for the making of roads, the discovery and development of mining and agricultural resources, and for the construction of various sorts of machinery and plant. Along with this productive work there goes a good deal of obstructive or destructive work, some of which is equally profitable to financiers. But the difficulty of disentangling the socially useful from the useless or noxious operations must not lead us to question the great importance that attaches to finance as a genuinely productive agency. Under a different social-industrial system much of this work might be dispensed with or done otherwise, but, as matters actually stand, the work of the financier is of immense value and must like other work be paid what is necessary to get it done efficiently.

This does not, however, imply that the profits taken by financiers are an accurate measure of the services they render or a minimum inducement to their rendering. On the contrary, there is no sort of work more likely to be overpaid. For the nature of these financial services frequently excludes effective competition. The floating of loans or the financing of big·companies can only be undertaken by a few great houses or groups, and the conditions of close bargaining, so as to drive the profits to a minimum, seldom exist. There is no market price for such work : it is a matter of special opportunities and special terms. The secrecy or semi-secrecy which enshrouds many of these financial operations also favours excessive payment. There can, therefore, be no question but that the profits of this class of business contain a larger proportion of unearned or unnecessary income than any other sort of profit.

It will be convenient here to present a summary of the results of the inquiry, made in this and the three preceding chapters, into the respective claims made by land, labour, capital, and ability upon the industrial pro- duct, and into the methods of enforcing these claims. The common interest of all parties concerned requires that out of the product, or income, as it is produced, proper provision should be made for the maintenance of each factor needed to carry on the process of production. Where anything is taken out of the land in the way of fertility of soil or other natural powers, it must, where possible, be restored : the land must not be let down. Proper provision must be made for wear and damage to buildings, machinery and other instruments, and for the risk of having to replace them by better sorts of instruments. Along with these depreciation and insurance funds for land and capital must be placed such part of the wages of labour and ability as goes to maintain the various sorts of productive human powers required to continue the work of production.   A part of wages and salaries will thus be classed not with rent and interest but with " wear and tear " provision.

These are all the payments necessary to secure the existence and continued operation of the industrial system as it stands. In a primitive industrial society they might exhaust the product, but under modern conditions the co-operation of the factors yields a product far in excess of what is needed for mere maintenance. This excess or " surplus " may be used to feed the growth of the industrial system by a properly apportioned distribution, or it may go as wasteful overpayment to the owners of any factor strong

enough to take it. A large part of the surplus does go in the shape of minimum interest
and profit, and wages of progressive efficiency,
to evoke larger and better supplies of the
various sorts of capital, ability and labour,
required in a progressive industrial society.
The state, too, requires and obtains similar
allowances for maintenance and a growth,
obtained by payments made out of the industrial product which the public services have
assisted to produce.

The whole of the industrial product, the
general income, could advantageously be
applied to these purposes of providing for
the maintenance and proportionate growth
of the factors of production. But it is evident that the whole of the surplus need not
be, and in fact is not, so applied. Much of
it is paid, not as provision for maintenance
or growth, but in excess of what is necessary
for these purposes. Going to landowners as
rent, to capitalists as excessive dividends, to
business men as excessive profit, sometimes
to workers as excessive wages, it retards
industrial progress. It takes portions of
wealth which might have been applied to
promote industrial growth and pays them as
" unearned income " to persons who thereby
not merely are not induced to increase their
output of personal energy but are enabled and
induced to diminish or withhold such pro-

F

ductive energy as they might otherwise have given out. For all unproductive surplus acts as an endowment of idleness.

This " unproductive surplus," whether obtained by owners of land, capital, ability or labour, is obtained in the same way, viz. by establishing a shortage in that factor and rackrenting the owners of the other factors. A natural or contrived monopoly or scarcity is the origin of every overpayment. It is manifestly false to attribute to one of the factors the sole power to take this surplus. Neither the landlord, nor the employer, nor the capitalist, possesses this exclusive privilege. Sometimes one, sometimes the other, finds or makes his factor " scarce " and gets a " pull " proportionate to that scarcity. In thickly populated countries the landowner takes a large share of this unproductive surplus in rising site-values and in agricultural and mining rents, except so far as easy and cheap access to large external supplies of foods and other materials qualifies his pull. In sheltered industries, where the possession of some natural or organized advantage gives certain capitalists the power to keep out " free " capital and to restrain free competition, capital may take its " pull " in high dividends and business men in high profits. Since such shelter and the scarcity it brings are usually achieved by the genius, skill, industry or luck, of business men, the proportion of such industrial gains which rightly ranks as profit is probably much larger than that which ranks as interest. A conjunction of trade-unionism and favouring circumstances occasionally gives a group of wage-earners a short-lived pull, enabling them to secure some unproductive surplus in their wages. In every case this unearned and unproductive surplus is the result of a natural or contrived shortage of one factor of production in relation to the others whose co-operation is required for the production of some sort of wealth.

CHAPTER IX

EXCHANGE AND PRICES

WE are now in a position to understand why a ton of kitchen coals in London may be bought for the same sum as will buy a pair of medium quality blankets, a britannia metal teapot, half-a-dozen cotton shirts, or forty loaves of bread. If each of these purchases can be made for a sovereign, it is because the various expenses of production, the payments to the owners of the different productive agents in the successive processes through which each of the articles has passed happen to add up to this same amount. In each case the sovereign contains a great number of little bits of price paid for the labour, ability, use of capital and land in the farming, mining, manufacturing, transport, distributive businesses, required to produce and put on to the market the ton of coals, the blankets, the teapot, shirts and loaves. If we traced each from its earliest stage and followed the raw materials as they moved through these processes, we should see the aggregate expenses mounting up until the retailer's profit completed the amount. At any of these stages we should find that the total expense of the productive process consisted of a variety of little expenses for the different sorts of labour, capital, land, ability required, some of these expenses bearing minimum or " free competition " costs, others being loaded with some " surplus " representing the monopoly or scarcity of some one or other factor.   The different articles selling for a sovereign will not by any means be composed of costs and surplus in the same proportions. It might be the case that the 20s. paid for a pair of blankets contained only 4s. or 20 per cent. of surplus (little rent or surplus profits being involved), whereas the 20s. paid for the loaves might be loaded with 8s. or 40 per cent., the rent of wheat land, a corner of wheat, a millers' or a bakers' combine, going to swell the final sum. It would require a special study of the history of each commodity to enable us to say how much of the final price the consumer had to pay for it was " cost " and how much " surplus," or again, taking the surplus, how much of it was productive, making for industrial growth, how much unproductive, i.e. wasteful or detrimental.

It has been sometimes held that " rents " and other surplus do not enter into and increase the final price of commodities, that they are only extra payments which owners of particularly advantageous land or capital can get. But our analysis, which identifies a " surplus " with a shortage and an enhanced price of the entire supply of some sort of land, capital,etc.,required in a process of production, disposes of this objection. For where there is a natural or contrived scarcity of any supply of productive power, the whole of that supply, whatever sort of standard measure is applied to it, rises in price. If hop-land is short in supply the price of hops will register that shortage. The fact that some acres of hop-land are better than others, and that the worst acres may get little more rent than they could get for growing wheat, does not affect the fact that the " scarcity " of hop-growing land raises hop prices. Of course what is called the " differential " rent, measuring the difference between the hop-growing power of a good and a bad acre, does not enter or affect the price. Why should it ? The price, like every price, is paid for a given quantity of commodity or service. If one acre gives out twice as much of this productive service as another, of course it is paid twice as much in rent. This has nothing to do with the " surplus " or " scarcity " element that enters into the price of a unit of hop-growing power.

Or, if oil or steel rails fall under a combine

or other business arrangement, limiting the number of wells or mills allowed to work, and restricting the market supply of oil or rails, this scarcity will raise the price of *all* the oil or *all* the rails, that produced by the worst wells or the most inefficient plant equally with that produced by the best wells or the most efficient plant. The real profits made by the worst wells or mills will, of course, be lower than those made by the best, but only because they give out a smaller quantity or a worse quality of output in a given time.

All the sorts of surplus which we have traced, taken by landowners, capitalists, employers, etc., in any process, extractive, manufacturing, transport, commercial, professional, financial, go to enhance the final price of the commodities purchased by consumers.

If there were absolutely " free competition " everywhere and equal abundance of all the factors of production, all prices would stand equally at a minimum, and all goods and services would exchange according to the sum of their " costs." Our blankets, teapot, shirts, bread and coal, unloaded of all their composite surplus, would, of course, no longer sell for a sovereign each, but at various lower levels. Some writers in Political Economy construct a theory which assumes this freedom of competition and this complete fluidity to exist, and then make allowances for " friction " or exceptions. But this, as Ruskin pointed out, is like starting the study of human anatomy on the supposition that the body is absolutely elastic and afterwards making allowances for its actual inelasticity. Scarcity and combination are as real and as normal features of the actual situation of our industry as are competition and abundance. In fact it is impossible to give any intelligible account of the working of the system without a doctrine of shortages and surpluses.

In our explanation of Markets and Exchange a clear comprehension of this fact is essential. Goods and services exchange against one another in proportion to their expenses of production or loaded costs, not in proportion to the quantity of labour-time they contain, or any other measure of " natural " costs of production.

The price, and therefore the expenses of production, of every portion of a supply of goods are the same. But the costs of each portion are not the same. The " costs " of growing a quarter of wheat are less in a fertile field than in an infertile one : the " costs " of producing 1,000 tons of steel are less in a well-equipped than in an ill-equipped works. Since " costs " *plus* surplus compose expenses, this implies that the surplus element in

expenses and supply price varies, being
biggest in the best type of business (farm,
factory, mine, etc.), smallest in the worst.
If one took account of all the farms growing
wheat for a particular market, one might
find a farm which it only just paid to put to
wheat-growing. That means that, in the
co-operation of land, labour and capital
which went to the raising of a quarter of
wheat upon this farm, more productive power
of labour and capital had to be bought to
make up for the smaller quantity of land-
power which was available. The same expenses of wheat-growing per quarter were
incurred in this farm as upon the better
farms, but a larger proportion of the sum
went as " costs " in paying capital and labour,
a smaller proportion as " surplus " in paying
land.

Similarly in the case of steel rails. Here
the worst plant in the industry corresponds
with the poorest wheat-farm. A larger proportion of the price per ton for steel rails
will go for wear and tear and maintenance
of capital and labour in the worst establishments, " profit " standing at a minimum.
In fact, the " expenses " of a ton, represented
by its price, say 30s., will be virtually absorbed
in these necessary costs, leaving no surplus
interest for investors or profits for the *entre-
preneur*.

F 2

But if there are some farms contributing
to the supply of wheat which only just
remunerate the capital and labour, leaving
no surplus for rent, how can it be said that
rent enters into price, enhancing it ? If
some establishments contributing to the supply
of steel rails only just pay their way and yield
no surplus profits, how can it be said that
there is any surplus element in the expenses
and the price of steel rails ? The answer is
that the scarcity of good wheat-lands is the
cause of the high average expense of raising
a quarter of wheat, enabling landowners to
charge a high price for the fertility of Nature
and loading the " costs " of labour and
capital with this surplus. The fact that
some land used is so infertile that Nature
contributes very little to the production of
a quarter of wheat, labour and capital doing
nearly all the work, does not affect the argument. If there had been plenty of fertile
land available, the surplus (rent) would be
very little, and the expense and price per
quarter would be so much lower.

It is this scarcity of better land that brings
worse land into use, by loading expenses of
wheat raising and prices with so large a surplus
that capital and labour can be employed re-
muneratively upon some poor land.

Similarly, the scarcity of well - equipped
steel-mills causes the average expense of

producing steel rails to be higher than it would be if there were an abundance of such mills, and by the high prices resulting from this scarcity a few worse-equipped mills are enabled to survive and just pay their way. The well-equipped mills will sell rails at a high profit, the ill-equipped mills will only cover costs. But all the same, the surplus profit which the scarcity of best plant enables the well-equipped mills to earn is represented in and is got out of the high expenses and price of rails : it is these prices, thus determined, that enable the few backward mills to keep on working.

This argument means that supply prices are not determined, as has sometimes been contended, by the costs of production of the most costly portion of the supply, i. e. the wheat produced in the worst land, and the rails turned out by the worst-equipped mills. This " marginal " land, as it is called, and these " marginal " mills are made just worth working by the fact that the scarcity of better land and better plant has loaded the expenses and the supply price with a surplus measuring the degree of that scarcity. Discover a new large rich wheat country, most of this surplus or " rent " that has entered into expenses and raised prices of wheat will evaporate, and with the fall of prices the bad wheat-land will pass out of use. Set up a lot of new

well-equipped steel plants, the scarcity value
of the existing plants will collapse, profits
and prices will fall, and the ill-equipped or
" marginal " mills will be driven out of use.

Expenses of production and prices of supply
are not, then, determined by the worst or
most costly businesses, but by the ordinary
standard business. In most staple manufacturing industries the vast bulk of the
production is done by establishments of
approximately equal equipment. Almost all
the mills or factories in a trade will have
up-to-date machinery and methods, and will
tend towards a common size or pattern.

In competitive trade, in order to hold its
own, a business must enjoy the same advantages as its competitors in buying its materials,
in working them up and in selling the product.
So in each of the staple textile or metal
industries there emerge from competition
one or two types and sizes of business more
effective and economical than any others, and,
since all the new capital put into the trade
runs into those shapes, they may be taken
as representative firms. It is the expenses
of production in these representative firms,
which do the bulk of the trade, that determine the supply prices of the goods. There
may be a few firms in the trade enjoying some
special advantages or economies in the shape
of patents or secret processes or management,

and so able to produce a little better or more cheaply than the representative type. There may also be a few firms of backward or obsolete type, with old-fashioned machinery or methods, struggling for their life and doomed to early extinction, unless they can be reconstructed and brought up to date. But these few superior and inferior firms will not appreciably affect expenses and prices. The representative firms, producing, say, 90 per cent. or more of the total supply, will regulate the prices. Superior firms will thrive upon these prices, enjoying high profits : inferior firms will starve upon them. When it is said that yarn or cotton cloth of a particular quality costs so much to produce, or that steel rails, rolled desks, wine-bottles, etc., can be turned out at such and such a price, it implies a reference not to the best and most prosperous business in the trade, nor to the inferior firm that barely pays its way, but to the normally efficient business.

There will, of course, be many trades where the variety of products and of processes is so great, and the changes of method so refined and numerous, that it will be difficult to find a standard type. In such trades as the chemical, electrical apparatus, motor car, there will be many sorts of product enjoying special markets within the general market, and produced by businesses which are undergoing transformations. But though here it may not be possible to point to any single or few normal business types, it will none the less be the case that expenses and supply prices for these classes of goods will be determined by the representative rather than by the exceptional business. The price of chemicals, electric lamps, motor cars, will be based upon the expenses and the competition of ordinary, big, well-equipped businesses.

Even in agriculture, where the variety in size and sorts of businesses seems illimitable, the same principle holds good. When an English farmer tells us that wheat cannot be grown at a profit when the price is under 30s. a quarter, he means that a good-sized farm employing modern machinery and with reasonably good management and labour in an ordinary season will make a living profit for himself by growing wheat for sale at this price. There will, of course, be farms with special advantages that will make a bigger margin of surplus out of wheat at such a price; other farms will still be unable to make it pay. The normal farm, in size, equipment, working, management, is always in the farmer's eye when he says that farming can or cannot pay with wheat at such a price, although he may not be prepared to explain exactly how he arrives at this normal farm. When one comes to special sorts of farming, such as fruit-growing, poultry-farming, etc., the business type becomes more clearly marked, although a great variety of ordinary farms may also contribute to the supply.

So far as capital and labour are able freely to enter any trade and compete for business, this competition will tend to select one or a few best types of business into whose hands will fall the bulk of the trade, and which will determine the ordinary expenses of production and the supply prices in the markets. If competition in these trades yields to combination, and trade agreements, pools, or trusts come in, it will still be these representative businesses that will determine prices, so long as the bulk of the supply remains in their hands. By restricting output they may raise " expenses " so as to include a large surplus-profit. But it is they who will regulate the market prices, not the starving independent firms outside the ring. These latter will usually " accept " the " ring " prices, making what they can out of them. So when the Standard Oil Trust raises the price of oil per gallon, or the Sewing Cotton Trust the price of thread, small outside producers generally raise their prices too, instead of exposing themselves to danger by under-cutting. As trade information becomes more rapid and exact, reaching a larger number of producers the standardization of sizes and methods of production gains ground, and the number of competing businesses which vary from the approved models becomes smaller. Of course it will always remain ,rue that exceptional ability and management or some special advantage in patents, access to raw materials or markets, will enable some particular firm or group to suck high profits out of the ordinary market price determined by their representative competitors.

If, however, these exceptional firms use their full business opportunities, they will gradually acquire a larger proportion of the trades. For, combining with strong trade rivals, they will force weaker ones to come in upon their own terms, or will crush them. When by these means they have formed a combination strong enough to enlarge or contract the whole supply of the market as they desire, they can fix selling prices so as to load costs of production with a large monopoly or surplus element. They do not, we repeat, need to absorb the whole trade in order to possess this power. A " trust," producing 50 or 60 per cent. of the supply, may sufficiently control output and prices, provided the outsiders are small and uncombined. Even if in some sections of its market there is effective competition at lower prices, other sections may yield monopoly conditions.

The economic origin and supports of such trusts, combinations and agreements are familiar. Sometimes they are rooted in access to the best, largest or cheapest supply of raw materials or power. Such is the basis of the De Beer's diamond trust, and the United States Steel Corporation derives much strength from possession of superior ore and coal. Sometimes railroad or other facilities of transport enable them to market their goods more cheaply than competitors. Such was the historic origin of the Standard Oil Company. Sometimes the possession of public favour or privileges, in the shape of tariff aid, public contracts, licences or charters of monopoly, is the main source of strength. Many companies for local services, e. g. gas, water, tramways, electric lighting, etc., come into this class. Large size of capital, reputation and special knowledge, have in certain instances enabled businesses to attain local or even wider control of markets. Perhaps the most conspicuous example of businesses enjoying high profits from this source is afforded by the present state of banking in Great Britain.

There is a popular notion that in an age of capitalism, since the larger business in a trade is always economically stronger and more profitable than the smaller, it is only a question of time for the whole trade to pass into the hands of a few monster firms which, after trying to slaughter one another, will end by combining. Thus it is conceived will competition work itself out in all the industries, leaving a single trust or combine in complete control of the market, and able to dictate prices to the consumer. In a good many industries the modern development of business life seems to sustain this view. Modern machinery of manufacture and of transport and modern credit have in many trades made the survival of small businesses impossible, and have handed over the industry to a few giant companies. An increasing number of trades appear to be going this way, both in the staple manufactures, transport, mining, commerce and finance.

But for all that the generalization is unsound. A large proportion of industry does not exhibit this tendency towards concentration. Even in the textile and metal industries large numbers of little businesses survive. Some of them, indeed, are only semi-independent, being tied more or less firmly to larger firms whose minor wants they supply. But in every great industrial province are found numerous genuine survivals of the small business, worked in the home or the small workshop with no expensive machinery and power. The essential irregularities of human nature are largely responsible for such survivals. Where the personal need, or taste, or fit, is the basis of a demand, the routine economies of the big business are at fault. There is no tendency for a high-class tailoring or dressmaking business to grow beyond such reasonable size as will admit the keen personal control of a capable manager. In all the luxury trades, where irregularity of demand is chronic and where personal taste and caprice impose themselves, small businesses are found. Work of repair forms a basis of livelihood for many artisans, such as shoemakers, carpenters, blacksmiths, though the making of the original goods has passed under large business enterprise. In agriculture, in mining, and in transport, there are many kinds of work which are best and most profitable in small forms. The small farmer still holds his own for many purposes. In retail trade, though the monster store has made great inroads, the high-grade shop and the local shop for minor and for perishable goods widely survive.

Moreover, even where the economy of production on a large scale prevails, it does not follow that no limit can be set upon the advantage of size. Because a big business can 'produce more cheaply than a little business and so can undersell it, it does not follow that a still bigger business can beat the big business at this game. Even in those industries where the size of capital counts for most, there will be a maximum type which cannot be exceeded without damage. When a business grows in size and complexity beyond a certain scale, there will be waste of central control in the co-ordination of the parts which will outweigh the mere economies of size. After a manufacturing business has grown to a scale enabling it to buy its materials, to organize its labour, to market its produce and to obtain credit, on the best terms, any further addition to its size will weaken it and render it less profitable. This size of net maximum efficiency will vary widely in the different trades. In some trades it will only be reached by a giant business which in its growth has swallowed its competitors and stands alone in the market, a monopolist. But such trades are the exception not the rule, even in countries where a protective tariff favours them by isolating the national market. Mere advantage of size, unaided by natural or legal supports, very seldom suffices to put a business into the position of a monopolist, able to dictate prices to buyers.

The real risk to which consumers are exposed in modern industry is rather that of suspended or mitigated competition among a few larger businesses than that of a complete monopoly. The economy of big production seldom hands over a market to a single firm, but it often reduces the number of effective competitors to a paucity that enables them by agreements to regulate output and fix prices high enough to yield them a considerable surplus profit. A great amount of experimentation in methods of federation and agreement among big firms in the same line of business is continually going on, and perhaps constitutes at the present time a graver menace to the consuming public than any domination of the " trust." The metal and machine-making trades, for instance, in Great Britain and America, are riddled with agreements for regulating selling prices, while shipping and railroad, insurance and banking companies, are continually forming " combines," " conferences " or other associations for regulating services and prices. Wherever one turns in modern industry, combination shows itself as real and almost as pervasive a force as competition. Now, since the prime motive and meaning of all these forms of combination is the acquisition of " surplus " profit, it is evident that no survey of market prices, or rates of exchange between different sorts of goods and services, can ignore the loading which these surpluses involve.

The history of every stock of goods exposed in shops for sale, if thoroughly investigated, would show that, at various stages in their

handling, the expenses which they accumu-
lated contain pieces of unproductive surplus
that, entering into the market price at some
earlier stage, are handed on to the later
stages with fresh accretions, so that in the
final shop-prices cost and surplus are inex-
tricably intertwined, the proportions between
the two differing in all the various kinds of
articles.

CHAPTER X

REGARDING the industrial system as a machinery for the production of wealth, we have naturally been led to find the origin of that wealth in raw materials which, passing through the various productive processes, gather value or importance from the work which is put into them, until as finished commodities they pass out of the machine into the hands of consumers. The growing quantity of work which they embody is represented in a continual growth of expenses and of price as the goods near completion, these expenses containing the sum of all the costs and surpluses entering at the different stages of production.

This picture of raw materials and goods constantly absorbing productive energy and expenses as they flow towards consumption, ignores, however, the controlling part exercised by the consumer. The end and aim of this application of productive energy is the satisfaction of the wants of consumers.[1] We have

---

[1] This general truth, like most others, needs qualifying. Some productive activity is desired on its own account

already seen how the money paid over the retail counter for commodities, circulating up the stream of production as payments for the various productive agents, continually stimulates the output of productive energy. By this demand for commodities the will of the consumer controls and regulates the entire system of production. That system exists to furnish him with "utilities." To him the commodities he buys are storehouses not of productive costs but of utility. The raw materials and goods in their various stages of production take all their value or importance from the final part they are to play as means of utility or human satisfaction. The machinery and other instruments of capital are similarly endowed with a utility from the consumable commodities whose production they assist. The whole of the industrial system can be regarded, from this standpoint, as an arrangement of goods and instruments containing various sorts and quantities of utility.

The utility of which we here speak is not the intrinsic worth of things, their " values " in Ruskin's sense as yielding true vital service by their consumption. It merely measures the actual current satisfaction which consumers impute to various sorts and qualities of goods, not the satisfaction they " ought " to impute to them if they understood their true interests. Thus a sovereign's worth of raw whisky must, for our present purpose of scientific analysis, be deemed to have the same utility as a sovereign's worth of bread or " best books." It is the actual desires that are operative. But a mere desire for " utilities " and commodities containing them has no effect. In order that a desire may be " effective " it must express itself through purchasing power. The unsatisfied needs and desires of poor people for goods that are beyond their meagre incomes have no economic, though they may have a deep social significance. The only utility that counts expresses itself through the use of actual incomes. The use of incomes, individual and collective, may thus be regarded as the final regulator of the industrial system.

In our business analysis we arrived at the conclusion that business men organized the various trades and businesses, actuated by the desire for profits. We have now to realize that these organizers and administrators are themselves the instruments or agents of the consuming public. For the business men, who by their demand for capital and labour determine how much of these productive forces shall go into this trade or that, are governed in their turn by calculations of the quantities of products they can market at a profitable price. Thus, in the last resort, it is the actual and expected demands of customers that really determine how much industrial energy of various sorts goes into the different trades.

The order and the disorder of industry, then, are mainly attributable to the will of the consumer operating through demand for commodities. It is to the urgency and importance of the different " demands " of the consumer that we must look for a chief explanation of the size of the different trades and the proportion of the productive force that they employ.

The simplest way of understanding the control of the consumer is to begin with a one-man system, the case of a Robinson Crusoe. How would such a man who had by his own efforts to supply all his needs dispose of his time ? His principal requirements are food, clothing, a hut and some tools and weapons. If the climate is tolerable, a certain minimum of food will rank first among his needs. An average of, say, two hours' work in hunting and preparing food, let us suppose, will give him that amount. If he wants more variety or quantity of food, and, not content with picking fruit and killing game, wishes to till a piece of land so as to raise crops, that will take a third and a fourth hour a day. But some clothes, though less urgent a need than the food obtainable by two hours' work, may be as desirable as the food which a third hour would secure and more desirable than that of a fourth hour. So he has to balance clothing against food for the use of his third and fourth hours in the working day. He can make and repair the barely necessary clothing in one hour a day, though two hours would give him a change in case of bad weather or damage. But a hut is nearly as essential as the first suit of clothes and more essential than the second. So he may decide to give only the third hour to making clothes and the fourth to making a hut. But a really commodious hut will take more than one hour a day to make and maintain. Shall he give his fifth hour also to hut-making? Some tools or weapons also have their claim. Shall they come in at this point, or only in the sixth hour of his working day, after two hours are given to hut-making? But the extra supply of food, postponed for the sake of clothing and a hut, may here again press its claim. He must evidently balance the three claims in his fifth hour, that of improvements in his hut, the making of an axe, or the laying in a further store of food. Of course the real problem will be a good deal more complex than this. There will be several sorts of food competing with one another for his time and energy. When he has got a certain amount of fruit, though he could do with more, he would prefer hunting for some flesh and fish.

So with the other needs, not only an axe but a spade, a bow, a hammer, are very useful: they also have claims upon his time. If he is a thoughtful man, he will adjust these various claims upon an economical principle, so as to make the best use of his working time. He will not go on making food when he has enough to satisfy his hunger, because though he could do with some more, the need of some clothing will assert itself more strongly. So with all the other needs, he will balance them against one another, so as to get the maximum of utility out of his day's work. He will stop doing each sort of work as nearly as possible at the point where any further product will be felt by him as slightly less desirable than some other thing that he could employ the time in making. At that second thing he will go on working until he has got as much as is quite necessary, and a third want becomes more urgent than an increased satisfaction of the second want. So far as he thus apportions his working time to the best advantage, it will be found that the last quarter of an hour which he gives to food is neither more nor less usefully employed than the last quarter he gives to clothes-making, to his hut or to making tools. For if we supposed the last quarter of an hour given to food produced a greater utility than that given to hut-making, it would be a wasteful use of time. So far as he consults clearly his best interests, he will arrange his different employments so that the last portion of the products of all of them are equal in the use or enjoyment they afford.

Now suppose that other people come and settle upon Crusoe's island, and he is able to get an income for himself by letting or selling desirable building sites. With this income he now satisfies his needs by setting other persons to produce various sorts of goods which he buys from them. The expenditure of his income will be conducted on the same lines as the expenditure of his working day when he worked for himself. Instead of laying out just so much time in making each several sort of food, clothes, house, etc., he will lay out just so much money. Part of his income he will spend on food, part on clothes, part on housing, etc. Though the first part of his food will have a very high utility, being the first necessary of life, the last addition to the food supply he buys will have the same importance or utility for him as the last addition to his clothes, housing or any other goods. Say that he spends £10 a year on bread, though the loaves he buys with the first five of these ten pounds have an enormous utility for him, the loaves he buys with the last pound could easily be dispensed with, and have neither more nor less utility for him than the last pound's worth of the £10 he spends on clothing or the last pound's worth of the £5 he spends upon cigars. The last pound's worth of loaves, clothing and cigars he buys must have the same importance or utility for him, so far as he lays out his income thoughtfully, for if we supposed the last loaves he bought to contain more utility than the last cigars, he would have acted irrationally and uneconomically in not increasing his expenditure on bread and reducing his expenditure on cigars.

So far, then, as a man uses his income economically so as to get the largest amount of utility from spending it, the last or least serviceable portion of each sort of goods he buys will have the same utility. Though he may estimate the total importance of his weekly supply of bread far higher than that of his weekly supply of tea, and the latter higher than that of his supply of tobacco, the last shilling he spends on bread must be deemed to furnish him the same quantity of satisfaction as the last shilling spent on tea or tobacco.

Now what applies here to the expenditure of an individual will be equally found applicable to the more complex expenditure of the income of a whole community. This aggregate income of the members of a community is spent partly in buying supplies of various sorts of foods, clothing and other prime necessaries or comforts, partly in buying innocent or noxious luxuries. Though it is evident that the first half of what is spent in foods and other necessaries provides far more utility than the first half of what is spent on luxuries, it remains true that the last or least useful portion of the bread, meat and other " necessaries " that is bought for consumption is just as much or as little useful as the last portion of any of the luxuries. The fact that the last portion of the bread supply *might have* a very high utility, if it could get into the homes of needy persons, is not here relevant. The last portion of the bread supply actually sold goes to swell the waste of the servants' hall in wealthy families, and gives out no more utility than the last box of cigars or the last bottle of champagne consumed in the dining-rooms of the same families.

If, then, we were to take the real income of this country, the supply of loaves, fish, flesh and fowl, the clothing, furniture, housing, jewellery, etc., turned out of the industrial machine in a year, we should find that the least serviceable part of each of these sorts of goods, when consumed, yielded the same amount of utility or satisfaction. For this balance at the bottom of each supply is rendered necessary by the consideration that consumers are always comparing and balanc-

ing against one another the different objects
of their desire in laying out the last portions
of the money they have to spend. As, then,
each individual gets the most for his money
by purchasing a number of supplies the last
portions of which represent to him an equal
amount of utility, so it will be with the
aggregate of individuals.

The objection will no doubt occur that,
with the very unequal distribution of incomes
among the various classes, a great waste of
aggregate utility will occur. For the loaves,
shirts, chairs, meat, which, forming the least
serviceable expenditure of the rich, have
least utility attached to them, might have a
high utility if they could have been purchased
and consumed by the poor. But that criticism, valid enough against the distribution of
income, does not impair the accuracy of an
analysis of utility based upon existing facts of
distribution. In considering the control which
the actual consumer exercises upon industry
through demand for commodities, it is important clearly to recognize the equalization
of utility at the base of each supply as the
immediate instrument for regulating industry.

In this levelling process of expenditure on
the part of a person or a society there is
nothing mysterious. It is simply " economy,"
the laying out of money or of effort to the
best advantage. Every child who, with a

shilling to spend, decides to spend twopence
on chocolates, threepence on shot, sixpence
on a cinematograph show and a penny on a
comic paper, performs this operation of comparing and equalizing marginal "satisfactions"
or "utilities." So far as the greater part of
expenditure is concerned, the process involves
no thought, it runs by routine. If a man has
an income of £500 a year, no question arises
as to how £450 shall be laid out. But as
regards the last £50, how much of it shall go
for holidays, how much for theatres, books,
subscriptions, how much for savings, that
will be a matter for some careful calculation
or individual adjustment. No two men with
£500 will spend the last £50 in the same way :
no man will distribute this expenditure in
the same way two years running. As with
an individual so with a whole society. Most
of the income of a nation, as of a person, is
by necessity or habit allocated to settled
expenditure in maintaining a standard of
consumption. Only the last portion, or any
increase of income, is subject to the process
of adjustment which we describe. This gives
great interest and significance to the last or
" marginal " portions of income in directing
changes of industry. The introduction of
a new luxury, the stimulation of a new taste
in a consuming class, will evidently cause a
flow of capital and labour into the industrial

G

processes which are needed to supply the article. The sudden direction of a large portion of the " spare " income of the well-to-do into a demand for motor cars has brought masses of new capital and labour into the trades providing them, has helped to make a rubber boom, and has injured the carriage trade and certain other luxury trades. So it is through all the grades of a society: new articles of consumption, music halls and skating rinks, cheap reprints, canned meats, bananas, popular drugs, force their way, first as casual claimants, then as habits, into the expenditure of some grade of the working classes, with important direct and indirect reactions upon the trades that supply them, or that supply other articles which they have displaced.

One is tempted to conclude that in these changes of taste or valuation which regulate the last items of expenditure are to be found the governing forces of industrial life. And great significance does rightly attach to them as indexes and instruments of economic movement. But it is a mistake to find in them the special causes or determinants of industrial change. For this would be to neglect two important considerations. In speaking of the new demand for motor cars we assumed that it originated in a new taste of rich consumers. But new inventions

and economies of production which put
reliable cars on the market at lower prices
stimulated and made effective this new
demand. And in most cases where a large
rapid increase of expenditure upon any
article takes place, improvements and economies of production have served to stimulate
the increased demand. In a word, there is
interaction between the forces of supply and
demand. A large cheap supply of cars stimulates an expansion of demand, expanded
demand stimulates a cheapening and enlargement of supply. So it is with almost all
economic changes. The same economy, the
same constant process of adjustment towards
an equilibrium, is taking place in production
as in consumption. The new or unappro-
priated capital and labour and ability tend
constantly to flow into those trades in which
some recent increase of demand has raised
the rate of interest, profit, wages, slightly
above the ordinary level of other trades, and
it goes on flowing until the increased supply
of products in the chosen trades, by lowering
prices, has restored the profit, interest,
wages, to the common level. The increased
supply and falling prices thus brought about
in the special trades in question, will cause
consumers to demand larger quantities of
these products and will extend their uses
to other grades of the consuming public, until

a new balance or equilibrium has been reached in the utility or satisfaction of the consuming public. Those disturbances and readjustments are always going on, alike in the costs of industry by inventions and improvements, and in the utilities of consumption by changes of taste and growth or decay of needs.

Another consideration is equally important. If we watched a number of tanks of water connected by pipes with one another, all the changes we saw would appear to be taking place at the surface, by a rise or a fall of that surface. If an additional supply of water were furnished to one tank, we should see the surface rising in each other tank in its turn until the common level was reached again. But though for observation and registration it would be best to confine our attention to the changes on the surface, it would be wrong to conclude that the causes which brought about these changes had any particular reference to the portions of the water on the top. For it might well be the case that the new supply of water to the first tank were made not at the surface but below, and that all the pipes connecting the tanks and causing the readjustment discernible upon the surface lay deep down. So in industrial changes both on the side of production and consumption the direct forces of change need not operate at the " margins," the least efficient portions of industrial power or the least pressing needs of the consumer. In industry some new general economy applied by all the representative firms of a trade, or a series of trades, some new economy of fuel, or the utilization of a waste product, will, by raising the margins of profit throughout the whole industry, regulate the distribution of the new capital and labour, so as to secure, as far as free competition exists, an equilibrium of profit among the various industries. So in the public consumption, the initial movement of change may be found not in the stimulation or expansion of some new taste just struggling into fashion, but in some alteration in the past standard of consumption in large sections of the public, as, for example, in a general weakening of the taste for alcohol, or a general rise of such an item as an annual seaside holiday in the scale of values of the large mechanic classes.

The changes at the margin, the readjustments of the least valued items of expenditure, of the least profitable items of industrial energy, are thus to be regarded rather as instruments for registering changes than as the determining causes.

What is supremely important is that students of industry should clearly recognize the methods by which the continual changes in the arts of industry and the valuations or taste of consumers alter the structure of the industrial system. These forces from the supply side and the demand side meet in what is called a Market, and their opposing tendencies are reconciled in the market price. A market price is that price which equalizes the rate of demand with the rate of supply, *i. e.* just enables all the goods offered in the market to find buyers. Take the instance of a cattle-market where a sale of bullocks is taking place. For simplicity we will suppose that all the bullocks for sale are known by all the parties concerned to be of the same size and quality. Some of the sellers are in urgent need of cash and would be prepared to sell a bullock at a low figure, say anything above £5. Some of the buyers are better off than others, and, being keener to buy, would pay a price as high as £12 rather than fail to get a bullock. Let us set out the market according to the number of willing buyers and sellers at different prices—

Price	No. of sellers	No. of buyers
£5	2	12
6	3	12
7	4	10
8	6	8
9	7	7
10	9	6
11	12	4
12	12	3

If the bidding begins at £5 there are only 2 bullocks offered at that price and 12 willing buyers, all willing to pay more if necessary. The market price evidently cannot stand at £5, for at that price 10 willing buyers would be left without a bullock, and to prevent being left would bid more than £5. They would first bid £6. But at that price there would only be 3 bullocks for sale and 12 willing buyers. The latter, still bidding against each other, would force the price to rise higher. At £7 and at £8 the same difficulty would remain. Though the number of bullocks offered and the number of willing buyers approached nearer, so long as there was one more buyer than there was bullock, he, fearing to be left, would bid against the others so as to raise the price. When this excess of buyers over sellers had thus driven up the price to £9, there would be found to be 7 sellers and 7 buyers at that price, *i. e.* supply is equal to demand. Could the price rise higher ? No, for at £10 there would be 9 sellers and only 6 buyers, and the competition of the extra sellers would force the price down to £9, just as the competition of the extra buyers had forced it up to that level. £9 is seen to be the only possible market price, for it is the only price at which the number of willing sellers and willing buyers is the same. So long as supply exceeds demand the price falls, so long as demand exceeds supply the price rises. The market price is at the point where supply is equal to demand.

This is true of every market where anything is bought and sold by processes of bargaining. Where buying and selling is continuous, as in most wholesale and retail markets for the sale of wheat, cotton or other produce, stocks and shares, or loaves, fish, shoes, coal or other commodities, it is not a fixed quantity of supply or demand that determines the price but the *rate* of supply and demand. The market price in London for wheat at any time will be determined at, say, 25*s.* a quarter, by the fact that at that price the rate at which wheat is offered at Mark Lane is equal to the rate at which it is being bought by millers and other purchasers. Where the market is a continuous process, Supply and Demand are to be regarded as " flows " measured over a period of time rather than as fixed quantities bought and sold at a particular time, as in our instance of the cattle market.

When Midland Railway Stock is said to sell at a firm price of 65, that means that for some time the number of shares offered at that figure continues to be the same as the number of shares bought.

Changes of price always mean an upset in

the equilibrium between the rate of supply and the rate of demand.

So long as the body of sellers in a market can go on selling their goods at the same pace as hitherto, they will not lower and they cannot with advantage raise the price. If they lower the price, they do so either because there is a fall off in the pace at which buyers ask for the articles, or because they have increased their stocks and wish by lowering prices to raise demand so as to meet the increased rate of their supply. If they raise their price, it is either because buyers are buying more frequently, or more largely than before, so depleting their supply more rapidly, or because they are finding a difficulty in getting a supply of goods at the same price as before. Thus the immediate cause of a rise of price is always a decrease of supply or an increase of demand : the cause of a fall of price is always an increase of supply or a decrease of demand.

Whenever the equilibrium between Supply and Demand is thus disturbed, the price continues rising or falling until a new level is reached where the two are again equal. This readjustment is a natural tendency. For if an increase in Supply has caused prices to fall, that fall will in itself stimulate an increase in the number of buyers or rate of demand. Similarly, if a decrease of Supply causes prices to rise, that rise of prices will reduce the number of buyers. The pace at which this tendency works will differ with different commodities. In some cases a small rise or a small fall of price will have a considerable effect upon demand. This will usually apply to luxuries, which do not satisfy any strong desire, or to articles for which there is a convenient substitute. In the case of necessaries or articles with no easy substitute a moderate rise or fall of price may be attended by little increase or decrease of demand. In the former case the " elasticity of demand " is said to be small, in the latter case large. The rise in the price of spirits, following the recent increase of liquor duties, caused a large reduction in the demand for spirits. A corresponding rise in price of wheat would not cause a corresponding reduction in demand for bread. It might even cause no reduction, so far as large classes of the workers were concerned. For the rise in price of bread might cause them to buy less meat or other foods, in order to be able to keep up their consumption of the staff of life. The effect which a rise or fall of 10 or 20 per cent. in the price of any article will have upon demand will evidently depend upon a great number of circumstances, and will differ in different social classes and grades of income.

Where the change of price is effected from

the demand side, similar effects will be produced upon rate of supply. In some cases an increasing sale will enable goods to be produced more economically than before, so that the rise of market price will be very slight and very temporary, resulting soon in a new equilibrium of demand and supply at a lower price than before. In other cases an increasing sale may stimulate supply only by causing a considerable rise of price, as where in order to create the new required supply worse land or dearer labour must be brought into use. According as supply does or does not respond easily to the stimulus of rising prices we speak of it as "elastic" or "inelastic."

All these important occurrences in the economic world which are said to affect prices work by means of this mechanism of Supply and Demand. A bad harvest, a new discovery of gold, a war, a rapid growth of population, a new invention for cheapening electricity, a temperance movement, affect prices, sometimes temporarily, sometimes permanently. But in all cases the *modus operandi* is to be traced in changes of the relation between supply and demand in the markets.

Most markets with their market prices are liable to numerous minor fluctuations from a variety of passing and casual causes. But behind or beneath these slight oscillations are to be traced large and abiding changes due to more important alterations in the arts of production or consumption. These normal or lasting changes in prices will arise from, or be expressed through, rises or falls in the ordinary expenses of production on the one hand, or in the ordinary utility of consumption upon the other.

Expenses of production will rise or fall either (1) by reason of some alteration in methods of production affecting costs, or (2) because of some increase or reduction in the " surplus " with which expenses may be loaded.

(1) Under alteration of methods of production will come (*a*) all those improvements in the arts of industry due to mechanical, chemical and other sciences, which are the leading feature of the Industrial Revolution; (*b*) improvements in business organization and enterprise, both on their productive and their commercial side; (*c*) improved skill, physique, education and character of the workers.

(2) Under influences affecting the " surplus " element we may include (*a*) discovery or development of natural sources of wealth, or the depletion of such sources causing increased scarcity and a larger surplus to arise in some necessary process; (*b*) an increase or decrease of the flow of capital into any country or any

industry, raising or lowering the expenses of production. This flow of capital is, of course, affected by innumerable causes related to the size and distribution of income, security of property, foresight, thrift and other conditions affecting saving and investment; (c) an increase or decrease of the flow of labour into the several countries and trades, determined by growth of population, facilities of information and of transport, and influencing division of labour and the labour-costs of production.

All these causes affecting expenses of production will impress themselves upon prices through enlarging or restricting Supply. Some of them, being of a general character, will affect most of the industries of a country, or of the world, though in different degrees, as, for instance, improvements in generating power for manufacture or transport. Others, being of a special kind only applicable to some trades, will raise or lower the expenses of certain products and affect their rate of exchange with other products.

Corresponding to these forces playing through expenses of production upon Supply are other forces, playing through utility upon Demand.

(1) An immense number of changes are always going on in the arts of consumption, *i. e.* in the utilization of the various forms of wealth. An improved fire-grate saving fuel,

a change in taste or habits of food or dress, a keener appreciation of books or recreation, and a thousand other changes, will result in increased or reduced demand for various commodities. New tastes and desires are constantly competing with and displacing old ones, and often by their adoption involve many other alterations in consumption and expenditure. The reduced use of alcohol, for instance, may involve less consumption of meat and a higher valuation for dairy produce and vegetable foods.

(2) Apart from such changes in tastes and habits, a mere increase or decrease in the size of the income of a nation or a class will bring about changes in the proportion of expenditure upon the various products. The general growth of income in large sections of our workers has expressed itself in an increased appreciation for holidays and amusements : the large growth of a " super-tax " class has brought an increasing demand for motor cars and other expensive luxuries.

Such are the forces which at every point of the industrial system are operating upon Supply and Demand to bring about the shifts of prices that are constantly taking place.

If we regard the Consumer as calling into being, maintaining and directing, by his needs and tastes, the whole of this great elaborate system of industrial forces, we shall see this Consumer's will operating everywhere through demand, first for commodities, and secondly for the various productive steps and instruments which are the necessary means to his end.

If, on the other hand, we take the standpoint of the business man, or Producer, we shall see the same structure and operation of the industrial system as a gathering stream of material and energy given out by various co-operative groups of factors of production, land, labour and capital, under the local guidance of business ability, moving towards the creation of quantities of finished marketable goods and services.

CHAPTER XI

THE LABOUR MOVEMENT AND STATE SOCIALISM

THE saying that all progress consists in the elimination of waste has a special applicability to the art of economic progress. It furnishes a test for the validity of the various methods of social-economic reform which play so conspicuous a part in modern history. In particular it can be seen that the Labour Movement on the one hand, and the enlargement of the industrial functions of the State upon the other, are virtually dependent on the existence of a surplus. It will be worth while to make this dependence clear.

If there were no unproductive surplus in the hands of capitalists, landowners and business men, the validity of the Labour Movement would hinge almost entirely upon the economy of high wages, short hours, and other improved conditions. For if the competition of employers and capitalists throughout the industrial system were everywhere so keen and constant as to keep down profits, interests, and other business emoluments at a minimum, any co-operative action of the workers, involving an additional cost of labour without a corresponding increase in the productivity of labour, would evidently prove disastrous for all the partners in industry.

In other words, the success of the Labour Movement would be confined to cases where higher wages, shorter hours, etc., raised the efficiency of labour so much as to involve no net increase in the labour-cost.   If this view were correct, all conflicts between capital and labour would be wanton acts of folly on one side or on both.   For if higher wages and improved conditions of labour of necessity were followed by a corresponding rise of productivity of labour, how foolish and inhuman for employers to resist such demands !   And how wrong trade unions would be to urge demands which, going beyond " the economy of high wages," could not be conceded by employers without ruining their businesses !

But the existence of a large composite surplus not required to maintain the other factors of production, but taken by them to be applied to purposes of luxury and waste, supplies a rational basis for the Labour Movement.   If the workers by organizing, alike in their several trades and as an economic and political unity, can secure portions of this surplus, applying it in the form of higher wages and more leisure to raise their standard of life and work, they are converting waste into genuine wealth. If trade-unionism, through collective bargaining, can secure higher wages, by reducing the payments made as rent, surplus-interest, and surplus-profit, no damage is done to the other factors, while an important contribution has been made to the improved efficiency of labour.

To this main object the policy of collective bargaining is directed. Its success, like that of other policies, depends upon the knowledge, skill and temper with which it is applied. Our analysis discloses many wide differences in the quantity of surplus available for distribution in the different trades. In some cases a large portion of the product goes as surplus-profit, or excessive interest, or is paid away in rents. This is the case where free competition has given place to combination among employers, or where some landowner, royalty-owner, patentee, or other monopolist, is able to rack-rent an industry. Other trades stand on a different footing, close competition among employers keeping down interest and profits at a minimum, and landlordism taking comparatively light toll. The same trade will at one time exhibit a large surplus profit, at another none.

The tactics of Trade Unionism consist in applying pressure at those industrial points where it can be applied with safety. An indiscriminate demand for higher wages, shorter hours, or any other condition involving a higher wage-bill, would prove injurious to industry and the injury would rapidly react upon the workers. For an industry where keen competition keeps down profit and interest to a minimum has no surplus capable of being applied to raise wages, and if by sheer strength of organization higher wages could be got, the trade may suffer damage in one of two ways. If foreign or other outside competition prevents the employers from raising the price of the product so as to meet the enhanced expenses of production, the trade will perish because no fresh capital will flow into it, and the wear and tear of existing capital will not be replaced. If it is possible to raise the price of the product, that rise of prices, as we have seen, must cause a shrinkage of demand, and this will mean a reduction of employment of labour which in its turn must damage the efficiency of the labour organization. The validity of collective bargaining as an instrument for raising wages, or shortening hours, clearly depends upon the directing and the timing of demands so as to secure for the workers the whole or part of some unproductive surplus ascertained to be in the possession of one of the other factors with which labour is co-operating. It is not the true interest of labour to seek to encroach upon such interest, profits, or other elements of income as are necessary to evoke the full use of other factors of production. But where any payment in excess of this amount is made, organized labour is economically justified in trying to divert this surplus into higher wages.

Whether, and to what extent, Trade Unionism can succeed in thus raising wages or otherwise improving the conditions of labour, at the expense of surplus-interest or profits, depends upon the relative strength of the organizations of workers and of employers. When a strong organization of labour has placed effective restrictions on the competition of " free " labour, it has often been able to bring such pressure on keenly competing employers as to raise wages at the expense of surplus interest or profit. But where employers have organized to meet such pressure, placing restrictions in their turn upon the inroads of " free " capital entering their trade, they have usually succeeded in defeating the pressure of organized labour. For their smaller number, larger resources, and better information, render their organization more effective in a conflict. Even in skilled and well-organized departments of labour there is a growing recognition of the inadequacy of Trade Unionism as a method of securing for the workers a sufficient share of the surplus wealth. Moreover, it is made continually more evident that the very policy which strong trade unions must adopt to limit the inflow of " free " labour from outside renders it more difficult for lower-skilled workers to organize their labour markets, which are flooded with the labour excluded from entry into the higher grades of employment.

The recognition of these facts is driving the Labour Movement into politics. There is a disposition among the workers, who form the majority of citizens, to use the State in order to supplement trade union and other private co-operative and philanthropic efforts to raise their standard of work and life. Although history shows that the State has always been utilized for the economic benefit of any class which acquired political control or influence, virtuous citizens have always protested against the partiality and corruption involved in such use of politics, and now profess concern lest the working classes should injure both the State and industry by unwise interferences with private enterprise and with the rights of private property.

" Because landowners, manufacturers, and other business classes have in the past used politics for their own economic ends, making and administering laws, treaties or tariffs, and using the diplomatic and military forces of the State for their business purposes, that is no reason why the workers should, if they get the power, follow the same dishonest and misguided policy in the interests of their class." Such is the objection. In reply, it is often deemed sufficient to insist upon two points. In the first place, it is contended that where the working classes form, as they do, the overwhelming majority of the electorate, their voice and their interests may be considered as the voice and interests of " the people " in a country where majority rule is acknowledged. Secondly, it is contended that many or most of the demands which the workers would enforce through the State consist in the alteration or reversal of legal rights or other advantages secured by landowners, capitalists, and other business classes formerly in control of the State.

Now, though both these answers have some force, they do not suffice to meet the economic objection, that the wage-earning classes might use their political power to injure the industrial system and to check the growth of wealth, by a short-sighted endeavour to raise wages and improve the condition of labour at the expense of the propertied classes.

The only effective answer is to show that the demands which labour seeks to enforce by means of the State, though primarily motived by the interests of a class, are ultimately consistent with and conducive to the interests of society as a whole. This is not proved merely by pointing out that the workers are by far the largest class. It must be shown that the policy they advocate is not in the long run injurious to the structure of industry. Now the acceptance of the doctrine of an unproductive surplus undoubtedly supports this interpretation of the labour policy. For so far as it is accurately directed to convert portions of the unproductive surplus into increased wages and leisure and other improved conditions of labour, the labour policy can claim to be a social policy. By transforming unproductive into productive surplus, it makes for industrial health and growth. To divert rents or surplus profits into a fund for securing a fuller subsistence for wage-earners and for enabling them to acquire for themselves and their families a larger share of the comforts and conveniences of civilized life, with ampler leisure, recreation and education, is a double social gain. It enhances the amount of utility and satisfaction got from the income thus directed, and it promotes industrial progress by raising the efficiency of labour.

The contribution of a reasonable labour policy to a social policy is best illustrated by the struggle for the "minimum standard." Whatever be the exact form or contents of our conception of social progress, it demands as a first indispensable condition a solution of the economic problem of poverty. This problem is of complex structure, distinguishable into several strata. At the bottom it appears as destitution, and the slowly but surely growing recognition that the safety of society requires the abolition of destitution has brought the State at many points into sympathetic contact with the Labour Movement. Public opinion everywhere demands that preventive measures shall be taken by society against low wages, over-work, neglected childhood, insanitary housing, sickness, accidents, intemperance, unemployment, helpless age, adequate public remedies being substituted for inadequate and degrading private charity.

For this purpose a series of public health, educational, industrial and philanthropic provisions are in course of adoption by modern States, based upon two assumptions: first, that large sections of the working classes are unable, as individuals or by private co-operation, to make adequate provision against many injurious and degrading incidents of their economic situation; secondly, that it is a sound social policy to utilize the resources of the State to assist them in doing what they cannot do themselves. Free hospitals, old age pensions, fuller provision against unemployment, and wages boards are illustrations of several branches of this new State policy.

It is noteworthy that in all these services the State is supplementing or displacing recognized activities of the Labour Movement, and is being brought at several points into direct co-operation with that movement.

But security against physical destitution is no sufficient foundation for a civilized life. It is the interest of every society that all its members shall, in return for work rendered to society, enjoy an income sufficient to enable them to maintain themselves and their family in full physical efficiency, with access to all reasonable opportunities of general and technical education, and to such social intercourse, recreation and liberty of travel, as are needed for a good workman and citizen. Now modern statesmen clearly recognize that for the great mass of workers some or all of these socially desirable conditions are not attainable by individual or collective bargaining. Neither competition

nor combination in modern industry yields
to workmen any sufficient security for such
a standard of work and life as is required.
The State must supplement the labour policy.
It does so directly in two ways. First, it
imposes conditions of employment expressly
designed to regulate wages, hours or other
conditions in a manner favourable to the
workers. The Wage Board experiment in
Australia is the most advanced example of
a policy which in this country is at present
confined to a few selected " sweated " trades.
But State regulation of wages here applies
not only to the growing number of public
employees but to the large amount of private
industry affected by public contracts. The
policy here pursued is a definite recognition
that private bargaining does not secure conditions of labour conducive to the social
welfare. The great body of modern industrial legislation in Factory and Workshops
Acts, Employers' Liability, Shop-hours and
other regulative Acts, is an expression of
this fuller policy of protection for labour.
It is a piecemeal endeavour to build up a
standard of employment consistent with the
minimum demands of our current civilization.

It is reinforced by another body of State
regulations which, regarded from the standpoint of the workers, aim at improving their
standard of living. Under this head may

be grouped much sanitary legislation, food adulteration Acts, and other protection against dangerous goods and services, while free or subsidized education and recreation, including libraries, parks, baths and other amenities, may be brought under the same policy. The chief economic effect of these various public services is to enable the workers to make a better or a more economical use of their earnings than they could under a complete system of *laissez-faire*, and to furnish to them at the public cost certain services they could not otherwise obtain. Regarded from the special standpoint of the economic interests of the working classes, this double set of State activities is engaged in expending public resources to build up a minimum standard of health, knowledge, enjoyment, taste, character and conduct, for those classes who are unable to make an adequate provision for these things out of the income they earn by the sale of their labour-power. It is an elaborate indirect attempt to readjust the adverse conditions of the wage-bargain.

This is, of course, but a one-sided and partial interpretation of a wider social policy. For while some of this public work and expenditure has exclusive reference to wage-earners, much of it claims a fuller social bearing. Though the poorer classes may get most benefit out of public money spent on education, recreation and even sanitation, it will be rightly held that these services are directed and intended less to fill the deficiencies of a class than to protect and improve the social organism as a whole. When we approach the higher grades of State activity, such as higher education, the encouragement of science, literature and the fine arts, the expenditure upon transport or the æsthetic improvement of our cities, we recognize that the social policy is less and less identified with the interests of any class.

These State services, anti-destitutional, educational, developmental, together with those defensive services which consume so much of the revenue of most States, involve the expenditure of a large and growing public revenue. The provision of this revenue itself occupies a place of growing prominence in the art of government. The chief difficulty in this art of public finance arises from a defective understanding of the part played by the State in industry and therefore of its claim to revenue. The notion that the State exists merely to protect the lives and property of individual citizens, and that for the performance of this duty it is entitled to exact a contribution from each citizen, proportionate either to his means or to the protective benefit he receives from the State, still underlies the common conception of public revenue. The effect of this view has been to impose narrow limits upon' State activities, and to regard the greater part of the public revenue as derived from confiscation of the property of individual citizens.

At the present time the theory and practice of public revenue is slowly emerging from these misconceptions. On the one hand, we see most civilized States transgressing the old protective limits by engaging in a large variety of constructive measures for the development of the economic and human resources of the nation. On the other, we see a growing recognition of public revenue as an income to which the State has a right, on .the ground that public services have earned it. This latter doctrine is, indeed, as yet not accepted in its completeness, except as regards the public revenue taken in the ordinary way as profit or rent from publicly owned property or publicly administered industries. The rents of public lands, mines, or other estates belonging to the Crown, the profits of the Post Office, of a municipal water or tram service, are evidently public income on the same footing with the similarly earned income of any private corporation. Wherever the State or city performs a particular service and takes a price from the recipient, whether that price is paid retail, as in the case of the Post Office, or wholesale as by some annual rate or fee, the public evidently ranks with other businesses and has the same sort of right to its profit.

Of course the public may abuse the right, exacting a higher payment than it ought for what it sells. Being usually a monopolist, excluding or limiting private enterprise, it is often in a position to abuse its power of fixing prices. Many of the services it undertakes are for the supply of necessaries or primary conveniences of life, such as transport, water, lighting. It is therefore able to swell the public revenue by exacting what would be in a private business surplus-profit. Some States and cities practise this finance, using certain monopolies, such as salt, matches, tobacco, alcohol, as instruments of public revenue. This is sometimes denounced as if it were an abuse precisely on all fours with the similar exactions of a trust or other monopoly in the business world. But it is not. For there are two differences. The surplus-profits of a State monopoly, though unearned by the specific services rendered, go to a public income designed for expenditure upon socially useful services, whereas the surplus-profit of a private trust goes to swell an unproductive surplus of private individuals. Again, the high prices exacted by the State may be dictated by considerations not merely of public revenue, but of public order, as in the case of alcohol or explosives.

But when a public monopoly is made a means of exacting profits higher than the ordinary business rate, it must be admitted that this excess is of the nature of taxation and must be defended as such.   It is, therefore, to the new conception of taxation as the chief means of providing public revenue that we must turn for an understanding of the relations of the State towards the industrial system.   This new conception takes practical, experimental shape in the distinction between earned and unearned income, and in the insistence that the State has a right to share in the latter.   Indeed, it is evident that to elements of private income and property regarded as " unearned " every modern State is beginning more and more to look for the increasing revenue required to fulfil the larger modern functions of a progressive State.   The two conceptions react on one another.   The perception that there are " large unearned " sources of wealth to tap enables and incites modern States and cities to undertake new constructive services in education, housing, town-planning, " social reform," which were not formerly considered financially feasible.   This fuller realization, on the other hand, of what a State or city can and ought to do for the common good, incites governments to a clearer recognition and a closer scrutiny of " unearned " wealth.

The self-interest of governments is everywhere driving them to seek more public revenue from " unearned " incomes and property. Such finance, at any rate in countries where forms of representative government prevail, lies along the line of least resistance. Everywhere it is felt and seen that rents of land, profits and dividends from liquor licences and from other businesses which, escaping the full brunt of competition, are able to regulate output and selling price, contain large elements of gain which can be taxed without injury to the industries affected.

If it were possible to track down all sorts of unearned wealth to a single source, as do some of the disciples of Henry George, or even to a few clearly ascertainable and measurable sources, a fairly simple policy of securing such wealth for public revenue might be enforced. One of two methods could be adopted : nationalization or specific taxation. The first method would mean the acquisition and ownership by public authorities of the land, or of such portions as possessed any considerable amount of present or prospective land-values. The effective working of this ownership policy might also necessitate the public ownership and operation of railways, mines and quarries, and perhaps buildings, as being in such intimate connection with the land as to suck value out of it. Along with this would go the public ownership of other natural monopolies, the retail liquor trade, banking and insurance, the telegraph, telephone, and some other means of transport and communication, the chief municipal services, and perhaps certain of the distributive trades in which the arts of combination or adulteration were likely to be used by private traders to the public detriment. This limited State Socialism, though motived partly by other considerations, such as the defence of the consuming public against high prices or inferior qualities of goods or services, would be directed primarily to secure public revenue. It would furnish the State income from the ownership and operation of monopolies.

The other method would leave the land, the railways and other instruments of " surplus " income in private possession and use, but would secure for the State such share of the surplus as it required by direct taxation. Economists have agreed that taxes upon economic rents of land cannot be shifted, and that not only do they inflict no injury upon the socially advantageous uses of land, but they may be so applied as to improve those uses. What holds of the rents of land, holds also of other monopoly values. Since

H

the monopolist has usually fixed the rents or other charges for the goods or services he sells at the figure which he estimates will yield him the largest amount of revenue, he will not raise his prices in consequence of the taxation he is called upon to bear. For it will not usually pay him to do so. The taxation is likely to stimulate him to more economy in methods of conducting his business, as it stimulates the landowner to put his land to more profitable use. It will not induce him to restrict his output, or to withhold any personal service which hitherto he had given forth. This economic doctrine of the taxation of " monopolies " is generally accepted.

But the analysis of industrial processes set forth in this book indicates a much wider and more various application. For if it be the case that surplus income emerges not only from the possession of land or of some few definite "monopolies," but from a great number and variety of circumstances and situations which afford a scarcity value to some sort of capital or ability that has gained a " coign of vantage," the amount of "surplus " available for public revenue through taxation is greatly enlarged. The profitable fruits of business trusts, combinations, pools and price-agreements, the gains from corners or manipulation of markets, from tariffs, charters

or other public aids, from inventions or
superior business organization, from high fees
and salaries, are all in various degrees amenable
to the taxing policy. The fact that most of
these businesses or professional activities
involve a genuine output of useful personal
ability, though complicating the taxing
policy, does not affect the principle. The
incomes derived from them contain elements
of scarcity value, unearned elements which,
though not directly separable from the necessary wage of ability, or minimum interest
and profit, are nevertheless a proper object
for taxation. Some of them are as large
and more enduring than the incomes derived
from city lands or liquor licences, others are
fortuitous and fluctuating. But, forming as
they do a very large share of the unproductive
surplus, public policy requires that due
attention be devoted to them as a source of
public revenue.

Their complex character and the difficulty
of measuring them, however, render specific
taxation unsuitable. The variety, complexity
and aggregate size of these more shifting
" surpluses " furnish the true economic justification for general progressive taxation of
incomes and inheritances. All taxes liable
to fall upon any income which is a true cost
of subsistence or of growth, *i. e.* the efficiency
wage of labour, the minimum interest, profit

or other payment of ability, are bad taxes. For, by impairing the efficiency of a factor of production they injure the future production of wealth, and reduce the surplus capable of contributing to future public revenue. All taxation, therefore, should be confined to " unproductive surplus," taking out of it such revenue as the State can advantageously expend in the sustenance and development of the public services. The general income and inheritance taxes, which in most civilized states play a part of increasing importance, are the best instruments for securing this contribution. Their progressive graduation is defensible upon the ground that the proportion of " unproductive surplus " varies directly with the size of the income or estate. This supposition may certainly be accepted as valid. The larger the income or estate, the larger the amount of unproductive surplus it usually carries, and so the larger the amount it can contribute to the State without injury to the factor which received the income.

The difficulty of discriminating such " unearned " income from the " earned " incomes in which it is often incorporated, however, obliges the State to proceed in an experimental manner. Grave practical difficulties confront a State endeavouring to tax surplus out of large incomes. Concealment of income is often possible, and modern international finance makes it possible and easy for some sorts of "surplus" to dodge taxation by emerging abroad and coming home in disguise. As internationalism in business grows commoner, it will become exceedingly difficult for any state to proceed much faster than other states in the taxation of current income. Partly to avoid these difficulties, but more largely because inheritances are admittedly unearned by the recipients, there is a growing disposition to rely upon death duties more than upon increased income tax for revenue.

Financial statesmen have been driven along these roads of revenue more by considerations of financial opportunism than by the clear-eyed acceptance of economic principles. But it is particularly desirable for those who realize the necessity under which a modern state continually finds itself of needing increased revenue, to understand the proper sources of taxation and the rationale of the taxing process. Taxation is not a confiscation of the earned property or income of individual citizens, the product of their personal effort or ability. It is a means by which the State, as the representative of social activities and needs, asserts its claim to the income which society has earned by the various aids rendered to its individual members. The State collects its income through the taxes, and expends it, so far as it is rightly advised, in the defence, development and improvement of the services it renders to society.

CHAPTER XII

FOREIGN TRADE

A CENTURY and a half ago a band of British immigrants landing in North America made their way into an extreme southern part of the province of Ontario, where they settled down in a fertile valley traversed by a river, along the banks of which they built the clusters of log-huts that presently grew into a populous and prosperous village. The north side of the river had most of the better grazing land, and a creek running down from the neighbouring hills made it easier to work lumber on that side. But the south side had land more fertile for wheat and better protection for fruit and vegetables. There were specially favourable plots of soil on either side under the shelter of the hills, which took the fancy of some settlers, and other advantages of climate, soil or position, led to special sorts of cultivation and industries connected with them. A few smiths, carpenters, weavers, tailors, shoemakers, settled, according to personal convenience or family connections, on the north or south side of the stream.

Remoth from other settlements, this village, with its neighbourhood of farmers, lumbermen, etc., formed a virtually self-supporting industrial community. There was a bridge across the river so that persons and goods passed freely to and fro, and market arrangements enabled every special advantage of soil or position, or any special skill which some artisan or manufacturer might possess, to be most fully utilized for his personal gain and for that of the whole body of customers who were free to buy what he had to sell. Here was a simple example of the economy of division of labour on a basis of free exchange. It was evidently advantageous for the villagers living on either side of the stream that there should be the closest contact and the freest commercial intercourse over the bridge. Any one suggesting that the bridge should be broken down, or that a toll should be set up for persons and goods passing across, with the object of enabling each side to supply its own needs whenever it seemed possible to do so, would have been dubbed a lunatic.

Now it came to pass, after the American revolution had led to the establishment of the Republic, that a delimitation of frontiers between Canada and the new United States took place, in which the river passing through our village was a boundary line. Politically the village was cut in two. The inhabitants of the northern part remained Canadian citizens, obeying the laws and paying the taxes of Ontario as heretofore, the inhabitants of the southern part became citizens of the United States. In process of time the political severance would possibly affect the feelings of the two sets of villagers towards one another and lead to a diminution of social intercourse. But could it make that division of labour and that freedom of exchange, which were advantageous formerly, less advantageous ? Would it be any less damaging than before to break down that bridge, or to put a toll upon the produce which sought a market across the stream ? It would indeed be feasible, as it was before, to break the economic community into two, following the line of the river. But it would be just as evident that every person who had anything to sell would have only half the market he had before, while for everything he wanted to buy he was similarly restricted in the supply available to him. It might be possible for all the villagers to supply themselves with all they needed by dealing with neighbours on their own side of the stream, but they evidently lose their share of the natural advantages or special skill belonging to some villagers upon the other side, and the new restrictions on the market for the things which they are in a superior position to make rob them of

H 2

part of the fruits of their own industry.
Each villager manifestly loses, both as buyer
and as seller, by any impediment put upon
that free intercourse which existed before.

The political division does not affect the
true economy of industry. It was advantageous before that the young men and women
who grew up on the north side should be
perfectly free to take up land or a trade upon
the south side if a better opportunity presented
itself there than on their own side. Such
liberty of movement evidently led to a better
development of the whole district, an advantage in which all would share. Similarly, if
any thrifty farmer on the south had laid by
a sum of money and saw a better use for his
savings by putting up a saw-mill on the
north side, instead of starting some less
likely business on his own side, it would
evidently be detrimental to the interests of
all the villagers on either side to stop him
from this most profitable use of his capital.
For they would all gain more by the cheaper
timber his saw-mill would supply than by any
other use to which he could put his savings
through employing them upon his own side
of the stream. Under such circumstances
any interference with the free flow of labour
or capital is seen to be as injurious as any
interference with freedom of markets. For
the inhabitants of either or both sides to

adopt a law of settlement which kept the growing population to its own side of the frontiers, or restrictions upon the export of timber or machinery or other sorts of " capital," or by a tariff to prohibit or impede the importation of commodities which could be produced better or more cheaply on the other side, would manifestly be a suicidal policy.

If the villagers upon the north out of some mistaken patriotism adopted such a policy of exclusion, they could damage the villagers of the south. But they would damage themselves to a somewhat greater extent, because the costs of collecting the tolls, keeping out smugglers and administering the whole protective policy, would fall on them. Supposing, however, that they were so foolish as to attempt this economic separation, would the villagers of the south be well-advised in their turn to meet the injury inflicted on them by copying the exclusion policy ? Why should they stop northern capital which sought to come in and develop their resources from doing so, or stop skilled labour from crossing the stream to help northern capital in their advantageous work ? Why should they prevent their villagers from getting the better or cheaper produce which the northerners still sought to supply ? To follow the bad example of the north would be to double the injury for their citizens as well as for the others, and to saddle themselves with the same costs of administering the exclusive policy.

So long as the village was all inside Ontario, it was quite obvious that the fullest co-operation among all its members, by division of labour, freedom of markets and full liberty of movement for capital and labour, was conducive to the common welfare of the village as a whole and of each section of it. It might be true that the soil and other natural conditions were upon the whole much more favourable on the south than on the north, and that consequently the young labour and the new savings went chiefly to the development and settlement of that section. But it would be quite evident that the villagers who stayed on the northern side were not made worse off but better off, by reason of the fuller development of the better resources on the southern side, and that if any foolish sentiment had operated to keep their young labour and the savings from seeking more profitable employment across the river, they would have been heavy losers. Now this evident economy could not be reversed or even modified by the purely political event which split the little industrial community into two political communities. What was good business before would remain good now,

and any political interference with the liberty
of movement for men and goods would evidently injure business. For if either of the
sections of the village could be advantaged
by restrictions upon free movements of men
or goods, it might equally be argued that
further barriers between the two parts of
the north divided by the creek which ran
into the river would be serviceable, at any
rate to one part of the north, and this policy
of subdivision might be carried so far as to
make each street and finally each family a
self-contained individual community.

This illustration will suffice to set forth
the simple and sound doctrine of industrial
and commercial relations between nations.
What these two sections of the frontier village
are to one another, are also the two nations
to which they relatively belong, Canada and
the United States. If an unimpeded flow
of capital and labour and products is
advantageous for both sides of the divided
village, so is it for the two nations. And
what is true for Canada and the United
States is true for any other nations, whether
possessing a common frontier or not. The
inhabitants of every country benefit by the
freest possible intercourse with all other
countries, for in that way they can get most
wealth, utilizing most completely and effectively any special qualities of natural resources

or acquired skill they may possess, and sharing by exchange the similar advantages which the inhabitants of other countries possess.

The main currents of modern industrial life involves the increasing recognition of this truth. Enormous strides in modern industry and wealth are attributable to a constant increase in the fluidity of capital and labour and commodities. Local markets for labour and for goods give place to markets over larger areas : the suckage of labour into large industrial towns extends over the whole country : modern machinery of investments carries capital more easily over the whole range of national industries. But the flow does not confine itself to the limits of a single country or nation. The most striking feature of the last generation is the expansion of economic internationalism, the growing forces that are conveying capital, labour and commodities over the whole earth, so as to develop more fully the general resources of the earth, and to distribute them more advantageously for the inhabitants of the earth. About a half of the new savings made by citizens of Great Britain finds a more profitable use in other countries, and the new capital of France, Holland, Germany, and other advanced industrial nations, similarly shows a tendency towards increased employment abroad. Most of this capital has gone into railways and other developmental work, by which vast new tracts of land and populations in South America, and elsewhere, have been made accessible as growing areas for the world-supply of foods and raw materials, and as markets for manufactures. Much capital has also been loaned to foreign governments or to municipalities, and when the primary needs of backward countries have been met, foreign capital flows into their internal industries of manufacture and commerce. Along with this flow of capital has gone a flow of labour from the more congested, or less fertile, to the less congested or more fertile countries. As might be expected, the streams of capital and labour have generally taken the same direction, the flow from all the European countries into North and South America forming by far the largest instance of this economic internationalism. Not less significant has been the corresponding distribution of business ability, engineers, bankers, merchants, factory managers, planters, spreading in ever growing numbers over the industrial world. The common object and result have been to " standardize " the world, so far as the roads, the structure and equipment of cities and of the leading industries are concerned, and even to force up towards a common level the practices of honesty and efficiency for government and business life.

The actual increase of foreign trade and the growing relative importance of that trade for every country form an aspect of this internationalism closely related to the foreign investment and immigration upon which we have dwelt. Though Great Britain and a few of the continental countries are in advance of the rest, the inhabitants of every country in the world are becoming more dependent upon the inhabitants of other countries for things they want to sell and buy. Every year larger and larger quantities of goods flow across the national frontiers and seek purchasers in foreign markets.

Apart from the ordinary exchange of goods for goods, the flow of capital to which we have alluded involves a large quantity of import and export trade. Capital invested abroad goes out in the shape of goods, for we have no money to send out, and it is not money but money's worth in goods that foreign borrowers want. Investment of capital abroad, therefore, is only a large department of our export trade, implying the sale abroad of British engines, rails, machinery and other British manufactures, sent out either to the country where the borrowers live or to some other foreign land. It also involves imports coming into this country in payment of interest on the capital, and eventually in repayment of that capital. For these payments, too, will mainly be made in the shape of goods. A very large proportion of the foreign trade of Great Britain and of some other countries consists of this flow of capital abroad and the payment of interest in return.

But, apart from this, there is a growing interchange of goods passing by ordinary process of exchange between countries which are different in their resources and their industries and which find such exchange the cheapest way of getting what their people want.

This flow of the factors of production and their products across national barriers is going on at an accelerating pace, and has important results, political as well as economic. It binds members of different political communities more closely by bonds of plain business interest. The striking fact that the people of Great Britain draw not much less than one-tenth of their total income in interest from overseas investments is not rendered less significant by the knowledge that the great bulk of this income is enjoyed by a very small class of well-to-do people. For it means that one-tenth of "economic England," in the sense of the property owned by Englishmen, lies outside these isles, in various parts of the habitable globe. This means a powerful interest in the peace, well-being and progress of those foreign countries,

felt by those Englishmen who own this property and receive this income. When we
reflect that the growth of this cross-ownership
between members of different nations is
going on everywhere, and that as intelligence,
ease of transport, and security of government
increase, so will this cross-ownership increase,
we cannot fail to recognize it as the most
powerful material factor in internationalism.
As its chief direct effect is to make countries
better known and more accessible to one
another, it evidently lays the foundation for an
enlarged and more regular flow of ordinary
trade.

These broad world tendencies towards
internationalization of industry do not, however, work unimpeded. Political interests,
real or imaginary, impel governments in many
countries to place obstacles on the free passage
of persons or of goods from one country to
another. Considerations, partly social, partly
economic, have caused some new countries
to impose prohibitions and restrictions upon
immigration, so as to regulate its pace and
character. This has operated as a very
considerable check upon the flow of labour
from Asia into the United States and our
self-governing colonies, and to a less extent
upon immigration from European countries.
This policy has been motived partly by the

determination of the working classes in new countries to defend their standard of wages and of living against the competition of new-comers accustomed to a lower standard. Though economists point out that the usual effect of admitting such immigrants has been, not the displacement of native labour, but its elevation to a higher level of employment, and that the early development of the rich resources of such lands as British Columbia and North Queensland is impossible without the free admission of lower races, such arguments do not generally prevail. The restrictive policy is defended by political and moral considerations relating to the difficulties of assimilating and converting into good citizens large masses of aliens of widely different stock and habits from those of the existing inhabitants of the country. For these and other reasons considerable checks are placed upon that free fluidity of labour which seems conducive to world-industry.

Most modern states, partly for purposes of revenue, partly because they wish to keep their home markets for their home producers and to make their country as economically self-supporting as possible, impose restrictions upon the free importation of foreign goods. Some they strive to keep out, others to admit with duties which reduce their quantity and raise the price. The tendency towards periodic gluts under modern industrial conditions has impressed upon most nations the difficulty of finding sufficient markets for the goods their producers can turn out, and has led them to suppose that, by keeping their own markets to themselves as much as possible they were increasing the total quantity of market for their national trades. But this they cannot do. For there is no way of increasing either the total wealth or the total market of a country by impeding freedom of exchange. On the contrary, every impediment must diminish the average productivity and the reward of capital and labour inside the protected area, as was evident in the case of our divided village. It is only by looking at one trade at a time, or trade with one country at a time, or trade for a brief selected period, or by some other " separatist " and fallacious consideration, that protection can be made to seem a profitable economic policy to any nation. Certain favoured protected classes or industries can gain at the expense of others, but the wealth of the nation as a whole must be diminished. This consideration of wealth may, of course, be offset by some other consideration such as national defence or variety of occupation. But it is well to recognize quite clearly that any military or other object gained by a protective tariff must be paid for in economic wealth.

Much confusion of thought is due to the habit of speaking of nations as if they were trading bodies, and of citing records of imports and exports as if they were national balance sheets exhibiting the sales and purchases of nations. Nations are not commercial units. Germany, Great Britain, the United States, do not trade with one another, nor do they compete with one another to sell to other nations. Certain persons or firms in Great Britain sell to or buy from certain persons or firms in Germany or the United States, and *vice versa.* German firms compete with English firms for orders from other business men in England and Germany or elsewhere, but the competition of the German firms with one another, and of the English firms with one another, is more incessant and keener than that between firms of different nationality. Kent hop-growers fear the rivalry of Sussex hop-growers more than of French or Germans, and would benefit much more by their exclusion or taxation.

The false notion that nations trade is accompanied by the equally false notion that in the processes of so-called international trade the interests of the several nations are opposed to one another. This fallacy is attributable to that misconception of trade which lays more stress upon the selling than the buying side. Because business men in the same trade find themselves rivals in the markets where they meet, they wrongly conclude that trade is composed of warring interests. Yet this is manifestly false. Our analysis of the industrial system shows it as essentially co-operative, competition only serving as an instrument in the co-operative process. Only by isolating the selling side of a business does trade appear in essence hostile. For trade does not consist in buying or in selling, but in both ; it consists in exchanges between goods, which are only effected by the sale of one set of goods and the purchase of another. If an English business man buys goods from a German firm, he compels that German to buy English goods which would not otherwise have been bought, or to get some other person to do so. If an Englishman sells goods to a German, he compels some English firm to buy German or other foreign goods which would not otherwise have been bought. Exactly how this is brought about need not concern us here, but it is evident that, since money does not pass between the two countries to any appreciable extent, payment for goods passing from one country is taken in goods passing the other way. Since the gain of trade to every person engaged in it comes equally by selling well and by buying well, it follows that he gains most who has access to the largest and freest market for both purposes. And since a nation consists of a number of individuals whose interests thus lie in selling and buying freely in the world market, the policy is also the true economic policy from the national standpoint. A state, therefore, which prevents its citizens from buying or selling abroad as freely as at home, injures their economic welfare, reducing the aggregate wealth of the nation.

The tariffs, treaties and other trade policies which states adopt, regulating the trade done by their own subjects with the subjects of foreign states, have, however, an excessive importance attached to them. Considerable as their influence is in determining the import and export trade between certain countries, they are not comparable in power with the great economic tendencies towards internationalism which we have described. The real interests of investors, merchants and wage-earners lie in the direction of the freest possible flow of capital and labour and the freest possible exchange of goods, and the magnitude and variety of this economic intercourse between the different countries of the world are continually increasing.

One point relating to imports requires attention. It is sometimes held that import duties need not be considered impediments to trade, but that they are means by which foreigners can be made to contribute to our public revenue. The foreign goods will come in as before, paying a tax which will not raise their price but will be taken out of the profits of foreign producers, merchants or shippers. Now the validity of the contention can be tested by the general law of taxation derived from the distinction between costs and unproductive surplus. It is simply the question of the effect of taxing different sorts of goods. Whether the goods taxed are foreign imported goods or home produce makes no difference. If a tax is placed upon goods produced under such competitive conditions as keep prices at a level which only covers the ordinary costs of production, it cannot be defrayed by the producers. For it will check production, reducing the supply of goods and raising their price, thus throwing the burden on the consumer. This applies equally to domestic or to foreign goods. If, however, there are cases where imported goods sell at prices which contain a " surplus " over the necessary costs the foreigner can afford to pay. If his own Government has neglected to take advantage of its prior opportunity to tax his " surplus," a foreign Government might do so by means of import duties. But only in such exceptional cases can the foreigner be made to pay.

CHAPTER XIII

HUMAN VALUES

OUR survey of industry shows us an elaborate system of businesses and trades by which the productive powers of Nature and of man are brought into operation for the supply of human wants. This system exhibits much detailed skill of adaptation and co-operation. The harmony of structure and of working in an ordinary modern business, a factory, a mine, a bank, a shop, is very exact. Though the owners of the different factors of production in the business are mainly moved by considerations of personal gain, viz. the wages, interest, rent, profits they expect to receive, there is a sufficiently close and constant harmony of these individual interests to supply a sound business economy. Though friction causes some evident waste, and larger disturbances sometimes arise, the ordinary business works harmoniously and economically at most times.

When we turn to the group of businesses which form a trade, and to the series of trades required to supply some sort of commodity to consumers, we still find a remarkable amount of accurate adjustment. If we consider the enormous number of minutely divided activities required to furnish London with any of its food supplies, the working of the industrial machinery appears marvellous. But here closer inspection shows much greater irregularity and waste. Twenty businesses are often engaged in doing the work which ten, or even five, could do as well; congestions and temporary stoppages of considerable magnitude occur; there is a good deal of miscalculation and of misdirected energy. The economy of a trade structure is evidently less exact than that of a business. The needs of humanity require, however, that a great variety of trades shall produce, carry, and distribute innumerable goods in the proper proportions simultaneously and continuously at ten thousand different places. We have seen how this is achieved by the establishment of an industrial system which sets the required quantity of land, capital, labour and ability in operation at each point of industry, and causes the new flow of capital and labour to repair the waste and to provide for growth. Few of the millions engaged in such work know or care at all for the larger purpose which this work serves. The farmer in Argentina or Alberta, who is

preparing bread for families in Manchester
or Dresden, is not consciously concerned
with any step beyond his bargain for delivery
of the wheat at the elevator or the nearest
railroad.

As we pass from the single compact business
to the wider system, less and less clear conscious purpose appears to animate the
system. And yet, as we see, a good deal of
order emerges in the working of the whole.
This order, however, is attended also by a
good deal of disorder. The modern industrial
system as a whole does not exhibit anything
like the same degree of harmony or economy
as is found in the single business. This is
natural enough. For we saw that in the
business a single control existed and a single
dominant purpose, that of profit-making.
Now in the industrial system as a whole there
is no adequate central control or purpose.
To a large extent, indeed, finance constitutes
a sort of central power station for the distribution of capital and labour. But its
grasp is very partial, and its methods are not
accurately adjusted to supply the general
needs of industry. The central purpose, as
we see, is the regular supply of the needs of
consumers. And it is this purpose which
does maintain such harmony as is found in
the industrial system. But the elaborate
circuitous ways by which the interests of

the consumer operate through the veins of industry are a poor substitute for the keen interest of the profit-maker in the organization of the business cell. No conscious controlling motive of social profit-making animates the whole.

Some indication of the nature and some of the extent of this harmony and discord has been given in the distinction between costs and surplus which our analysis disclosed. So far as costs of maintenance for the various factors of production* was concerned, we recognized that the industrial system worked almost automatically and accurately. With regard to costs of growth, though there was an ultimate harmony of interests between the factors, present considerations of gain caused discords to arise, a scarcer and therefore stronger factor encroaching upon the fund needed for the growth of some other factor, and taking for itself some surplus-gain. The needs and claims of the State, we also saw, were liable to similar depredations on the part of a powerful factor of production.

The discord and waste thus caused was not, we saw, measured merely by the quantity of surplus-wealth thus taken. For a proper distribution and utilization of the whole product would maintain a larger volume of production, giving full regular employment not merely to the existing industrial structure but to a structure enlarged by a better apportionment of nutriment to the separate parts.

A first line of social-economic reform is suggested by such analysis. The absorption and social utilization of the whole surplus, by converting the unproductive surplus into a productive service for labour and the State, would secure for industry as a whole a harmony resembling that which prevails in a well-ordered single business. Though the owners of the several factors of production, and the several businesses and trades, would each continue to endeavour to secure for themselves the largest payment, the economy of distribution which prevailed would keep them working together in economy and harmony. This is the ideal which *laissez-faire*, operating on a false basis of unequal opportunity, has often claimed but always failed to secure.

But in no case could mere self-interest of the separate factors, however enlightened, suffice for social harmony in industry. For we have seen that such a harmony of individual interests leaves out of account the claims of society, as an organic whole, expressed through the State. Now society, we recognize, must be considered as co-operating everywhere with the individual owners of land, labour, capital and ability, and as entitled to a regulative voice in industry and to its share of the industrial product. This truth is everywhere finding expression in the enlarged economic activities of modern States. Though there is no general tendency or conscious policy vesting in the State the ownership and operation of all industries, the State in every civilized country is entrusted with growing regulative powers over private industry, designed, first, for the protection of its members, as workers, consumers, or citizens, against risks or injuries incident to profitable processes; secondly, for the direct participation of the public in the wealth which social as well as individual energies have helped to produce.

The complete measure of State Socialism is commonly applied only to such economic processes as, left in private hands, tend either to become monopolies, or to breed dangers or disorders which defy mere regulation. To these are added, in some countries, trades which are made convenient instruments of public revenue. Though the economies of modern capitalistic production, and growing facilities of combinations of large businesses drive an increasing number of trades into this condition of monopoly or defective competition, qualifying them for public enterprise, it cannot be concluded that these concentrative forces are of universal

or of general application. Moreover, even
in cases where they operate powerfully, the
public policy in dealing with them will be
determined by the capacity of the State to
undertake in the public interest the conduct
of such industries. Where the State feels
competent to undertake an industry, or
where the difficulties of mere regulation seem
too great, full socialization will occur. But
when the State does not possess the requisite
strength, skill or integrity, the social interest
may be better secured by regulation and
participation in the surplus profits of the
trade. The particular industries subjected to
one process or the other will vary with the
degree and character of economical and
political development attained in the several
countries. But everywhere the State, as a
social instrument, will be found playing a
larger economic rôle as manager or regulator
of industry and as participator in the income
which it yields.

The essential meaning and value of these
processes lie in their contribution to the
wider and more human art of wealth. This
aft of wealth they further in two ways. By
removing from private income unearned and
excessive elements which by their payment
and expenditure represent waste, and by
applying such income to socially serviceable
uses, they impart increased health and vigour

to the industrial system and enlarge the
aggregate of satisfaction it affords by the
consumption of the product. By establishing
a more adequate central direction over
industry, commensurate to its increasing
complexity, they abate the waste of friction
due to conflicts of interest among individuals
and groups, and make for the production
of a maximum of human utilities with a
minimum of human costs.

www.ingramcontent.com/pod-product-compliance
Lightning Source LLC
Chambersburg PA
CBHW020852270326
41928CB00006B/664